CALIFORNIA
COOKING

Editor:
Betty Nowling

Creative Editor:
Rue Byars

Food Editor:
Karen Berk

Associate Food Editor:
Joan Burns

Photographs by
Michael Skott

Text by
Lois Dwan

Styling by
Jeanne Skott

Food Styling by
Andrea Deane

PARTIES,

CALIFORNIA
COOKING

PICNICS & CELEBRATIONS

by the
**Art Museum Council
Los Angeles County Museum of Art**

Clarkson N. Potter, Inc./Publishers
DISTRIBUTED BY CROWN PUBLISHERS, INC., NEW YORK

Grateful acknowledgment is made for use of the following recipes:

"Greek Walnut Torte with Brandy Buttercream Icing" from *With Love From Your Kitchen*. Copyright © 1976 by Diana and Paul Von Welanetz. Reprinted by permission of J. P. Tarcher, Inc.

"Madame Wong's Shanghai Shrimp in Shell" from *Madame Wong's Long-Life Chinese Cookbook*. Copyright © 1977 by S. T. Ting Wong and Sylvia Schulman. Reprinted by permission of Contemporary Books, Inc., Chicago.

"Veal Medallions and Onion Marmalade" from *Modern French Cooking for the American Kitchen*. Copyright © 1981 by Wolfgang Puck. Reprinted by permission of Houghton Mifflin Company.

Recipes copyright © 1986 by Los Angeles County Museum of Art Photographs copyright © 1986 by Michael Skott

Manufactured in Japan

Designed by Gael Towey

Library of Congress Cataloging-in-Publication Data

California cooking.

Includes index.
1. Cookery, American—California style. 2. Entertaining. 3. Menus. I. Art Museum Council (Los Angeles County Museum of Art) II. Nowling, Betty. III. Skott, Michael. IV. Dwan, Lois.
TX715.C15143   1986   642'.4
86-9470
ISBN 0-517-56083-6
10 9 8 7 6 5 4 3 2

ACKNOWLEDGMENTS

This book is a celebration of California—the foods as well as the diverse lifestyles and landscapes. The menus and recipes are eclectic—a blending of the new with the traditions of the past. The book is a result of a blending, too, of the efforts of talented volunteers from many different parts of the state. It began when Patsy Glass, following the success of the Art Museum Council's first cookbook, *Entertaining Is An Art*, inspired and led a group of Council members in the collecting and testing of favorite recipes for a second cookbook. Patsy set the standards of excellence that have guided this project, and we are most grateful to her. We are also indebted to Sue Labiner, whose insight was invaluable in forming the book's present concept, and to Max Eckert who was so generous with his professional assistance at this time.

We wish to gratefully acknowledge Tappy Hunt, who enthusiastically assisted with the complicated logistics of location and photography. We express much gratitude to the magnanimous home and yacht owners who opened their doors and allowed us to capture a photographic glimpse of how they live and entertain. We thank those who helped to select these sites and assisted during the photographing. We gratefully acknowledge those who gave so freely of their recipes and the committee members who tested them. The testing committee spent hundreds of hours cooking, tasting, and retesting, always with a joyful spirit.

We are also deeply grateful to the innovative restaurateurs and other food professionals who gave us inspiration and guidance, and shared their recipes with us: especially chef Gerry Gilliland of Gilliland's, for contributing a traditional Irish menu; executive chef Didier Lenders of The Lodge at Pebble Beach, for most generously planning two menus to showcase the foods of the Monterey Peninsula; chefs Bruce Marder and Bill Hufferd of the West Beach Café and Rebecca's, who contributed the extensive and innovative menu for the Mexican fiesta; cookbook writer Judy Zeidler, who contributed bread recipes; and Judy Chroman, wine judge, who recommended the California wines to complement our menus.

We are indebted to John Hubbard of the Irvine Ranch Markets, who contributed the exceptionally beautiful food that was prepared for each meal, and to his staff, who showed us many courtesies during the six weeks that we shopped, cooked, and photographed. The same generous spirit was shown by merchants throughout California who so willingly supplied flowers, dishes, and accessories for our tables.

This book is possible only because of the generosity of everyone listed here and in the credits on page 224, as well as many who are not listed. Our thanks to all.

Betty Nowling, Rue Byars,
Karen Berk, and Joan Burns,
Editorial Committee

CONTENTS

CITY

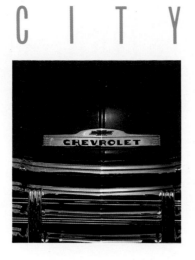

MOUNTAINS

INTRODUCTION

California cooking began in the mid-seventies, when a remarkable group of very talented young chefs discerned the kernel of truth in French nouvelle cuisine. Led by the late Jean Bertranou in Los Angeles and Alice Waters in Berkeley, they set upon a course of principled experiment that exploded into a galaxy of tastes as brilliant as the French Impressionists' explosion of color.

The most recognizable characteristic of this new cooking is freshness, closely followed by natural tastes. Flavors come forth as beautifully unadorned as Botticelli's *Venus*. Sauces are meant to enhance, not to conceal.

There are reasons why this happened first and differently in California. It follows, if natural flavors are to be starred, they must be the finest and most interesting flavors, and for that California is superbly suited. The climate is mild, the soil is fertile, and the ocean teems with seafood. If we do not yet produce all the foods of the world, the chances are we will, and that they will thrive. We have been a wine country for a long time.

California is the frontier, the Far West, close enough to be influenced by the centuries-old culinary philosophies of the Orient. We still have the venturesome spirit of the pioneer. We are more easily persuaded to try the new, more inclined to run wild with our enthusiasms.

The French were our first teachers. We also learned—and are still learning; it is no completed thing—from the Chinese, Thais, Japanese, Italians, Vietnamese, Koreans, Mexicans, and anyone else within range of our curiosity.

When nouvelle cuisine lost its beginning common sense and fell into disrepute, the jeering symbol was the kiwi. But la nouvelle did not have to do with anything as concrete or particular as the kiwi. When I asked Paul Bocuse to explain it, he said, "Simplicity." When I asked Jean Trois-

gros, he said, "It is freeing the chef." In California, the chef was not only given his head, but very quickly, a crown to put on it. He was not only free, but a hero.

California cooking has become more than skill, more than sensuous awareness. It is a recognition of the meaning of food that sounds all through history and echoes in the pleasures and ceremonies of our own lives. We have learned to break only the best bread together. We have decided that the quality of what we eat matters to us very much.

This book is an unusual effort by members of the Art Museum Council of the Los Angeles County Museum of Art. All accomplished cooks in their own right and experienced hostesses, they have documented the California home cooking that developed from the restaurant cooking of the chefs.

The menus, which have been composed from the point of view of the artist as well as the chef, show an uncommon matching of food to place and occasion. The settings are glamorous, and glamor—as well as practicality—informs the recipes. The homes were chosen for aesthetic reasons—some for their art treasures, some because they were exemplary of a period or a style, some for architectural imagination. The natural locations are not only beautiful, but particularly beloved by Californians, who live outdoors as much as they do indoors.

This book will give pleasure not only to Californians, but to any adventurous cook. "Food is life," says Andre Simon. "...But food can and should also be fun; it has in its gift some of the joy that makes life worth living."

Lois Dwan

Santa Monica, California

OCEAN

California curves its lean length along the Pacific Ocean as though it were a lover, which, in a sense it is—a benevolent, moody, dominating lover that can be neither ignored nor resisted. Those who cannot live within sight of the sea make pilgrimages for a day, or a week, or a summer.

The Pacific has been a major influence on the history of the state, its style of living, and the development of California cooking. There is the obvious abundance of seafood, of which the following menus make good use. All along its 1,264 miles of coastline, commercial fishing boats, divers hunting abalone and mussels, patient fishermen sitting on piers, and sportsmen out for the deep-sea big ones, can be seen at almost any time.

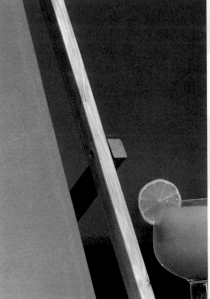

The ocean controls the climate, too, to the benefit of wine grapes, as well as fruits and vegetables that cannot grow elsewhere in this country.

The Pacific has always seemed to attract venturesome people, those who are naturally curious about the food they eat, and eager for a new experience. People who might experiment, for example, with roasting a whole salmon in a pit dug in the sand, just for the fun of it. (One menu gives the how-to.)

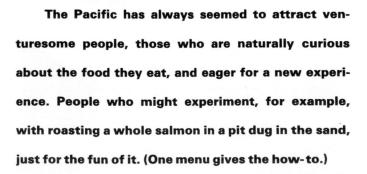

LAGUNA BEACH

Laguna Beach perches on a ledge between the cliffs rising dramatically behind it and the drop to a broad sweep of white sand and breaking waves. It is a dreamy seaside village, its charms fiercely protected by the inhabitants. Artists are encouraged; many seascapes are painted here. The Pageant of the Masters, a living re-creation of great paintings, is an annual event, drawing an audience from all over the southland to a surprisingly moving experience. But mostly, Laguna Beach is content.

The secluded cove chosen for the barbecue was alive with all the action of a sunstruck day at the beach. Windsurfers swooped and glided across the blue waters like giant, bright-colored birds or winged dancers. Red, blue, and yellow Frisbees sailed high and ever higher. Guests gathered yellow mustard flowers for the table, which was set in the sand.

There is no better way to prepare a comely fish than to wrap it in seaweed and bury it over coals. The Indians who once roamed these shores and gathered most of their subsistence from the teeming waters knew this, and so does the modern, beach-loving Californian. At this beach picnic the digging of the sandpit for the salmon provided high drama. The activity was good for the guests' appetites, and there was plenty of time later for a swim and a cool drink.

There is no doubt that salmon reigns supreme on the Pacific Coast. It is a different genus from the Atlantic salmon, but not inferior—except to Easterners. We love ours and they love theirs, but it is hard to believe anything could be better than a fine Chinook properly prepared.

COOKOUT IN THE SAND

FOR **12**

Bucket of Crudités with Chunky Dill and Garlic Dip

Peppered Corn Soup with Cornmeal Croutons

Salmon Cooked in a Sandpit

Sliced Tomatoes with Sun-Dried Tomato Vinaigrette

Rye Salt Flutes

Orange Torte

Ice-Cold Beer or Pinot Blanc

. . . .

Crudités with Chunky Dill and Garlic Dip

Some crudités—like asparagus and broccoli—benefit from a brief blanching. Others—like the carrots, celery, green peppers, etc., chosen for this picnic—are fine as is. Jicama, that crisp, sweet, juicy tuber from Mexico, is wonderful.

- 4 **hard-cooked eggs, chopped**
- 2 **to 3 tablespoons finely chopped fresh dill**
- 1 **tablespoon dry mustard**
- 4 **medium garlic cloves, crushed**
- 2 **to 3 tablespoons freshly squeezed lemon juice**
- 1 **teaspoon anchovy paste**
- 2 **cups mayonnaise, preferably homemade (page 176)**

Combine all ingredients and mix thoroughly. Refrigerate overnight to allow the flavors to blend. Serve with assorted crudités.

MAKES ABOUT 2 CUPS

Peppered Corn Soup with Cornmeal Croutons

This is a rich soup; small portions should be fine, but the recipe can be doubled if desired. The corn for this soup should be as fresh as possible.

- 4 **tablespoons (½ stick) unsalted butter**
- 1 **cup minced onion**
- 2 **large garlic cloves, minced**
- 1½ **cups finely chopped leeks (white part only), thinly sliced**
- 3 **cups milk**
- 2 **cups heavy cream**
- 4 **cups fresh corn kernels (cut from approximately 6 large ears of corn)**
- 2 **cups chicken stock, preferably homemade (page 17)**
- 2 **teaspoons salt, or to taste**
- 1½ **teaspoons freshly ground black pepper, or to taste**

GARNISH
Cornmeal croutons (see Note)

Melt the butter in a large heavy saucepan and add the onion, garlic, and leeks. Cook over medium heat for 2 to 3 minutes, stirring often, and add the milk, cream, and corn kernels. Bring to a boil and add the chicken stock, salt, and pepper. Simmer for 4 to 5 minutes, just until the corn is tender. Serve hot, garnished with cornmeal croutons.

NOTE: To make cornmeal croutons, make one recipe Corn Bread (page 26), cut it into ½-inch squares, and toast at 350° for 10 minutes, until crisp. Store in an airtight container.

SERVES 12

Beautiful soup—made of
corn and cream and a
flash of black pepper—is
even more beautiful on a
beach when the sun
slides down and a chill
creeps in from the ocean.

Chicken Stock

Any good California cook has a supply of stock in the freezer. Reduced and frozen in ice-cube trays, it keeps nicely in plastic bags. One cube, reconstituted with wine or water, can be the magic ingredient of a hasty meal.

- **5 pounds chicken necks, backs, and wings**
- **2 medium onions, peeled and cut in half**
- **2 leeks (white part only), cut into 1-inch pieces**
- **3 carrots, scrubbed and cut into 1-inch pieces**
- **3 celery stalks with leaves, cut into 1-inch pieces**
- **1 bay leaf**
- **1 teaspoon dried thyme**
- **12 peppercorns**
- **8 sprigs of parsley**

Rinse the chicken parts under cold running water. Put them in a stockpot with enough cold water to cover. Bring to a boil, then reduce the heat to a simmer. Skim off the scum as it rises. When the scum stops accumulating, add the rest of the ingredients, return to a simmer (do not boil rapidly, or the stock will become cloudy), and cook, partially covered, for 2½ to 3 hours. Skim as necessary. Add boiling water if needed to keep the solid ingredients covered.

Strain out the solids and let the stock cool, uncovered (it will sour if covered before it is cool). Refrigerate, then remove the fat on the surface. The stock may now be refrigerated, covered, for up to 3 days, or frozen.

N O T E : Because stock is often used in a sauce reduction, salt has not been added.

MAKES ABOUT 3 QUARTS

The picnic table is set with white plastic-handled flatware and napkins that are really hand-woven dishtowels. An unglazed terra cotta vase is filled with wild mustard flowers, and a blue glass carafe holds a refreshing cooler (left). A variety of crudités with the dip (right).

Salmon Cooked in a Sandpit

Salmon (or any other large fresh fish) prepared in this fashion is worth the effort.

> **1** whole fresh salmon (6 to 8 pounds), cleaned and
> split lengthwise, head and tail left on
> **Salt**
> **1** to 2 medium onions, thinly sliced
> **2** lemons, thinly sliced

Approximately 1½ hours before cooking, prepare a mound of charcoal in a sandpit and start the fire. After 45 minutes to 1 hour, spread the coals to the length of the salmon. Continue to let heat for about ½ hour more.

Meanwhile, wash the salmon inside and out with cold running water and pat dry with paper towels. Sprinkle the cavity lightly with salt and fill with alternating slices of onion and lemon. Wrap the fish tightly in a double layer of well-oiled heavy-duty foil, folding the edges over 3 or 4 times to close securely. Make sure the coals are ash gray before beginning the next step.

With a shovel, remove and reserve all but a thin layer of coals from the pit. Place the fish on the thin layer of coals, cover it with the reserved coals, and insulate with hot sand. Leave the salmon in the pit for 45 to 50 minutes. Carefully remove the sand and coals and gently lift the salmon out of the pit, being careful not to tear the foil. Transfer the salmon to a serving platter, garnish with the cooked lemon and onion slices, and serve immediately.

VARIATION: Place the sealed foil package on a well-heated barbecue grill with the lid closed. Cook over medium hot coals for 45 to 55 minutes. Turn over midway through the cooking time, which will vary with the temperature of the fire. To test for doneness, insert a metal skewer through the foil, halfway into the thickest part of the salmon. Remove after 5 to 6 seconds; if the tip of the skewer is hot to the touch, the fish is done.

SERVES 12

Guests relax with a cool drink while the coals heat (right). The salmon waits for the fire, and (far right) done to perfection, is served in all its tempting glory with red, ripe tomatoes topped with sun-dried tomato vinaigrette.

Sliced tomatoes garnished with fresh basil waiting to be dressed with the vinaigrette.

Sliced Tomatoes with "Sun-Dried" Tomato Vinaigrette

For many years the roofs of the Italians in San Francisco have been bright with flat pans of tomatoes drying in the sun, but only recently did the rest of us learn their virtues. Their quite different flavor in this vinaigrette immeasurably enhances the ripe tomatoes—vine-ripened, if possible.

VINAIGRETTE
MAKES ABOUT ¾ CUP

- 6 whole "Sun-Dried" Tomatoes preserved in olive oil (recipe follows)
- 1 to 2 tablespoons diced onion
- 2 tablespoons red wine vinegar
- ¼ cup extra virgin olive oil
- ½ cup loosely packed chopped basil or cilantro (or Italian parsley)
- 2 tablespoons capers, undrained
  Salt and freshly ground black pepper, to taste

- 8 to 10 large (or 12 medium) ripe fresh tomatoes, sliced ¼ inch thick

GARNISH
Fresh basil or cilantro

To make the vinaigrette, drain the sun-dried tomatoes but reserve 2 tablespoons of the oil. Put the dried tomatoes in the bowl of a food processor fitted with the steel blade and process until finely minced. Add the onion, reserved oil, vinegar, olive oil, and basil or cilantro. Process until smooth. Stir in the capers and season with salt and pepper.

To serve, spoon the dressing over the sliced tomatoes. Garnish with fresh basil or cilantro.

SERVES 12

"Sun-Dried" (oven-cured) Tomatoes

Although sun-dried tomatoes are available in specialty markets, they can be dried in an oven at home very nicely. However acquired, they are delicious in a vinaigrette, as a garnish for many dishes, or with fresh mozzarella and olive oil.

Italian plum tomatoes
Salt
Extra virgin olive oil
Garlic cloves or bay leaf (optional)

Cut the tomatoes in half lengthwise. Using your fingers, remove about half the juice and seeds. Flatten the tomatoes slightly so that they will dry evenly. Sprinkle generously with salt. Place on a rack, cut side up, over a baking sheet or pan.

To cure in an electric oven, turn the thermostat to the lowest possible temperature and do not let it rise above 110° to 120°. (You may need to prop the oven door open to accomplish this.) In a gas oven, the pilot light should keep the temperature low and constant. The important thing is to dry the tomatoes rather than cook them.

Leave the tomatoes in the oven for 24 to 36 hours, depending on the oven and the size of the tomatoes. Check after 12 hours. When the tomatoes are done, they will be firm, with no liquid left. If removed before they are completely dried, they tend to be bitter.

Soak the dried tomatoes in extra virgin olive oil, making sure they are well covered. If desired, add whole garlic cloves or a bay leaf to flavor the oil for salad dressings.

The tomatoes in oil will keep for up to 8 months in an airtight glass container stored in a cool dark place.

Rye Salt Flutes

These crusty flutes, with a sprinkling of salt and caraway seeds, add a decorative touch to the picnic table.

    2   packages active dry yeast
        Pinch of sugar
    1   cup lukewarm water (105° to 115°)
    1   cup lukewarm milk (105° to 115°)
    1   tablespoon salt
    2   tablespoons unsalted butter, melted
    5   tablespoons caraway seeds
    1   cup rye flour
    4   cups unbleached all-purpose flour
    2   egg whites, slightly beaten
        Coarse salt

Dissolve the yeast and sugar in 1 cup lukewarm water. Let stand for 5 minutes. In a large bowl, combine the lukewarm milk, salt, butter, and 2 tablespoons caraway seeds. Add the yeast mixture and rye flour; blend well. Add the all-purpose flour 1 cup at a time, mixing well. Knead on a floured board for 6 to 8 minutes, until smooth. Place in a greased bowl, turn the dough to coat it well, cover, and let rise in a warm draft-free place for 1 hour. Knead; divide into 6 balls.

Using the side of your hand, pound the dough balls and shape into flutes, approximately 12 inches long by 1½ inches wide. Fold each in half lengthwise and pinch the seam. Place on a greased baking sheet (seam side down) and let rest, covered, for ½ hour. Preheat the oven to 400°. Brush the flutes with the beaten egg whites and sprinkle with salt and the remaining caraway seeds. Bake for 20 minutes, until the flutes are golden brown and sound hollow when tapped on the bottom. Let cool on a rack.

MAKES 6 FLUTES

Awning stripes of confectioners' sugar and an orange peel garnish make this a festive picnic cake.

Orange Torte

A fine, firm cake that can be eaten by hand, is not overly sweet, and has a refreshing taste of oranges—just right for the end of a day at the beach.

    2¼ cups (10 ounces) blanched almonds
    1½ cups sugar
     3 large navel oranges
     6 eggs
        Large pinch of salt
    1½ teaspoons baking powder
    1½ teaspoons almond extract

GARNISH
        Confectioners' sugar, sifted
        Candied Orange Peel (page 61) or
        additional orange slices

Preheat the oven to 375°. Grease and flour a deep 9-inch springform pan. Grind the almonds finely with the sugar in a food processor fitted with the steel blade.

Rinse the oranges. Place them unpeeled in a medium saucepan and cover with water. Boil for about 30 minutes, until very soft. Drain and cut into quarters; remove the rind, scraping away as much of the white pith as possible. Process the rind and pulp of the oranges in the food processor until finely puréed.

In a mixer, beat the eggs until thickened and light in color. Fold in the almond-sugar mixture, salt, baking powder, and almond extract. Fold in the orange purée. Pour the batter into the prepared pan and bake for 1 hour, until the cake is firm to the touch. Cover with foil if the cake begins to brown too much. Let cool in the pan on a rack. Remove from the springform, dust with confectioners' sugar, and garnish with candied orange peel or additional orange slices, if desired.

MAKES ONE 9-INCH TORTE

VENICE

This home is a bold experiment, entirely in the why-not spirit of Los Angeles. It was conceived by Robert Graham, a sculptor who had never before designed a house. With the collaboration of the owners he created a geometrically pure, uninterrupted, high-ceilinged space, then carefully added the work of other artists, challenging them to design tables, doors, windows, cabinets, fences, etc. The result is an extraordinary harmony of permanent, functional art, focused by Graham's own people sculptures.

Cubes and rectangles form the basic structure, with steps as a repeating motif and relieving curves in the furnishings. It is filled with light and detailed with art—frescoes, murals, mosaics, stained glass, and doors that are abstract paintings. It is a calm and caring house, meant for people. The big front window opens to make a terrace of the living area, admitting and becoming part of all the turbulence of Venice beach—the shouting children, the sailboats, the seagulls floating in for treats . . .

The house is happy with guests. Any number, from two to a hundred, can be accommodated with grace. The menus were planned to meet the challenge with simplicity, the drama of color, some uncommon juxtapositions, and a careful disregard for rules. There is a suggestion of the Middle East in some of the dishes, acknowledging the background of the hosts. Lunch was in the dining area, near the big open window, and supper was on the roof—very Mediterranean, with its banked flowers and vivid mosaics. The sun set just before the fog rolled in.

A salad bright with cantaloupe and snow peas (a-
bove), and scallion-flecked
shrimp artfully arranged
on striped white-on-white
plates (right). The mini-
ature bronzes are by
Robert Graham.

Sugar Snap Pea and Cantaloupe Salad

Shrimp in Mustard Sauce on Corn Bread Rounds

Pomegranate Sorbet

Chenin Blanc

. . . .

Sugar Snap Pea and Cantaloupe Salad

The Chinese brought the edible peapod to our attention, but combining it with the sweetness of melon and accenting the whole with the bitterness of watercress is California thinking.

**¾ pound sugar snap peas, strings
removed, cut in half diagonally**

CREAMY SHERRY VINAIGRETTE
MAKES ABOUT 2 CUPS

1 egg
2 tablespoons freshly squeezed lemon juice
2 tablespoons red wine vinegar
1 tablespoon sherry
1 medium garlic clove, crushed (optional)
½ teaspoon crushed dried tarragon
½ teaspoon anchovy paste
¼ teaspoon salt
   Freshly ground black pepper, to taste
1½ cups vegetable oil

**1 small cantaloupe, peeled, seeded, and
cut into slices ½ inch × 2 inches thick**
**½ bunch of watercress, stems removed,
cut into 2-inch pieces**

GARNISH
3 tablespoons slivered almonds, toasted

Blanch the sugar snap peas in boiling salted water for about 1 minute, until barely tender. Rinse immediately in cold water and dry well.

In a small bowl combine all the vinaigrette ingredients except the oil. Whisking constantly, add the oil slowly until well blended.

To serve, spoon some of the vinaigrette onto individual salad plates, and arrange the snap peas, cantaloupe, and watercress on top. Drizzle with additional vinaigrette and garnish with toasted slivered almonds.

SERVES 6 TO 8

Shrimp in Mustard Sauce on Corn Bread Rounds

Corn bread is more American than apple pie, and a fine homey foil for the shrimp. Leftovers are excellent cubed and toasted for croutons (see Note, page 14).

CORN BREAD ROUNDS
- 1 cup sour milk (see Note)
- 1 teaspoon baking soda
- 1 cup unbleached all-purpose flour
- 1 cup yellow cornmeal
- 1 teaspoon salt
- 2 eggs
- 2 tablespoons unsalted butter, melted

SHRIMP IN MUSTARD SAUCE
- ½ cup scallions, cut diagonally into ½-inch slices
- 2 tablespoons vegetable oil (more if necessary)
- 18 to 24 raw jumbo shrimp, shelled and deveined, with tails left on
- 2 shallots, minced
- ½ cup dry white wine or vermouth
- ½ cup heavy cream
- 8 tablespoons (1 stick) unsalted butter, cut into small pieces
- 2 tablespoons coarsely ground French mustard (such as Moutarde de Meaux)
- Salt and freshly ground white pepper, to taste
- Freshly squeezed lemon juice

GARNISH
- 12 to 16 scallions, cut diagonally into 4-inch lengths

To make corn bread rounds, set a rack in the lower third of the oven and preheat the oven to 450°. Generously butter an 11 × 17-inch jelly roll pan.

Mix the sour milk and baking soda in a small bowl. Combine the flour, cornmeal, and salt in a food processor fitted with the steel blade; mix well. With the machine running, pour in the sour milk, then add the eggs and melted butter, blending just until combined. Pour the batter into the prepared pan, smoothing the top. Bake for 10 to 14 minutes, until the bread shrinks from the sides of the pan and springs back when lightly touched. Let cool in the pan on a rack. Cut into 4-inch rounds.

Blanch the ½ cup of scallions in a large saucepan of boiling salted water for 2 to 4 minutes, until crisp-tender. Drain well and set aside.

Heat the oil in a large heavy skillet over high heat. When very hot, add the shrimp in batches and stir-fry for 1 to 2 minutes. They should be slightly undercooked. Remove with a slotted spoon and set aside.

Reduce the heat to medium, add more oil to the skillet if necessary, and sauté the shallots for 30 seconds. Pour in the wine, scraping up any browned bits, then stir in the cream. Cook for 4 to 5 minutes, until the mixture thickens and coats the back of a spoon. Reduce the heat to low. Gradually whisk in the butter, then the mustard. Do not let the mixture boil. (If you wish to increase the amount of sauce, add up to 1 stick more butter.) Add salt, pepper, and lemon juice to taste.

To serve, reheat the corn bread rounds in a low oven or toast until crisp. Put a round on each heated plate. Top each round with 3 shrimp, spoon on some of the sauce, and sprinkle with the reserved blanched scallions. Garnish with lengths of raw scallion. Serve immediately.

NOTE: To make sour milk, pour 2 tablespoons vinegar into a 1-cup measure. Fill with milk and stir lightly. Let stand for about 10 minutes, until curdled.

SERVES 6 TO 8

. . . .

Pomegranate Ice

Ices made with fresh fruit are beloved in California. Pomegranate pleases with its vivid color.

- 1⅓ cups water
- 1⅓ cups sugar
- 2⅔ cups pomegranate juice, freshly squeezed (see Note) or bottled
- ¼ cup freshly squeezed and strained grapefruit juice (preferably from Ruby Red grapefruit)

GARNISH
- Sprigs of fresh mint or fresh Ruby Red grapefruit sections

In a medium saucepan, combine the water and sugar. Bring to a boil, stirring until the sugar is dissolved, then simmer until clear. Set aside to cool. Combine the sugar syrup with the pomegranate and grapefruit juices. Freeze in an ice-cream machine according to the manufacturer's directions, or in metal trays (see Note, page 155). Serve within 12 hours, garnished with mint sprigs or grapefruit sections, if desired.

NOTE: To obtain juice from pomegranates, use a rotary citrus juicer. Strain the juice through cheesecloth.

MAKES ABOUT 1 QUART

The brilliant color of the pomegranate ice is enhanced by a sprig of mint and by the glass designed and made in California.

ROOFTOP SUPPER

FOR **6** TO **8**

Marinated Sea Scallops with Radishes,
Avocado, and Grapefruit

Cold Roast Tenderloin of Beef with
Pommery Mustard Sauce and Rémoulade Sauce

Couscous Salad on Kale • **S**esame Cracker Bread

Poached Figs in Port and Custard Sauce

Petite Sirah or Zinfandel

· · · · · · · · · · · · · · · ·

Marinated Sea Scallops with Radishes, Avocado, and Grapefruit

An elegant adaptation of the classic seviche of Spain and Mexico, adding the crisp bite of radishes and the contrast of grapefruit.

1 **pound sea scallops, each cut into 3 or 4 horizontal slices, or whole bay scallops**
½ **cup freshly squeezed and strained lime juice**
1 **teaspoon minced cilantro**
1 **teaspoon salt**
1 **teaspoon freshly ground white pepper**

VINAIGRETTE
2 **tablespoons red wine vinegar**
6 **tablespoons vegetable oil**
1 **garlic clove, minced**
¾ **teaspoon salt**
 Freshly ground white pepper, to taste

1 **grapefruit**
1 **large avocado**
 Freshly squeezed lemon juice
½ **cup thinly sliced radishes**

GARNISH
 Sprigs of cilantro

In a large, nonmetallic shallow bowl, toss the scallops with the lime juice, cilantro, salt, and pepper. Tightly cover and refrigerate for 6 hours or overnight, stirring occasionally.

Combine the vinaigrette ingredients in a glass jar. Shake thoroughly and chill.

To serve, detach grapefruit segments from the membrane and discard any seeds. Cut the avocado into chunks, or slice it, and sprinkle with lemon juice. With a slotted spoon, remove the scallops from the marinade and combine with the grapefruit, avocado, and radishes. Toss very gently with the vinaigrette. Spoon into individual serving bowls and garnish with cilantro.

SERVES 6 TO 8

A California version of seviche is dramatically presented in clear crystal bowls that catch the late afternoon sun on a rooftop ledge in Venice.

Cold Roast Tenderloin of Beef

A requisite of California cooking is using the best ingredients, and beef is a prime example. This dish demands the finest. Here *cold* does not mean refrigerated; the beef should be cooled only to room temperature for serving.

> Vegetable oil
> 3 to 4 pounds trimmed beef tenderloin, center cut, at room temperature
> Freshly ground black pepper, to taste
> Salt, to taste

GARNISHES
> Cherry tomatoes
> Pitted ripe olives
> Watercress

Preheat the oven to 425°. Heat oil in a skillet large enough to hold the meat. Rub the beef with pepper and sear on all sides for about 5 to 7 minutes. Remove from the skillet and place on a well-oiled rack in a roasting pan. Roast in the oven until a meat thermometer inserted into thickest part of the beef registers 125° for rare (25 to 35 minutes) or 140° for medium rare (35 to 40 minutes). Roasting time will vary with the thickness of the tenderloin, so use the thermometer to test for doneness. Do not overcook.

Sprinkle the beef with salt and let cool to room temperature. To serve, carve the beef crosswise into thin slices and arrange them overlapping on a platter. Garnish with cherry tomatoes, olives, and watercress. Serve with Pommery Mustard Sauce and Rémoulade Sauce (page 32).

SERVES 6 TO 8

With its white stucco walls, cascading flowers, and backdrop of blue water, this could be almost any Mediterranean rooftop. Couscous and cracker bread served with the tenderloin add to the Middle East feeling.

Pommery Mustard Sauce

This is an easy sauce. As an alternative, however, you might want to try fresh horseradish and sour cream, or jalapeño jelly melted in a little wine.

- **1 egg**
- **3 tablespoons Pommery or other whole-grain mustard**
- **1 tablespoon freshly squeezed lemon juice**
- **¼ teaspoon salt**
  Dash of Tabasco sauce
- **⅓ cup safflower oil**
- **3 tablespoons extra virgin olive oil**

Combine the egg, mustard, lemon juice, salt, and Tabasco sauce in a small bowl. Whisking constantly, drizzle in the oils until the sauce is smooth and thickened. Store covered in the refrigerator.

MAKES ABOUT 1 CUP

. . . .

Rémoulade Sauce

As with all rules, the classic recipes are often bent and modified to California whim. A classic rémoulade would have chopped gherkins, spring onions instead of garlic, and fresh chervil in addition to the tarragon.

- **1 egg yolk**
- **1 tablespoon freshly squeezed lemon juice**
- **¾ cup vegetable oil**
- **1 small garlic clove, finely minced**
- **¼ teaspoon freshly ground black pepper**
- **1 tablespoon minced fresh tarragon or 1 teaspoon dried**
- **1 hard-cooked egg, finely chopped**
- **1 teaspoon anchovy paste, or to taste**
- **1 tablespoon minced capers**
- **2 tablespoons minced fresh parsley**

Combine the egg yolk and lemon juice in a small bowl. Whisking continually, add the oil drop by drop at first, increasing to a thin steady stream as the mixture thickens. Stir in the remaining ingredients and refrigerate, covered, until ready to use.

MAKES ABOUT 1 CUP

Couscous Salad on Kale

Couscous is the staple of the Maghreb (the North African countries of Algeria, Morocco, and Tunisia), served at every meal and amenable to any embellishment—the more elaborate, the wealthier the home.

- **4 cups chicken stock, preferably homemade (page 17)**
- **6 tablespoons extra virgin olive oil**
- **¼ teaspoon turmeric**
- **¼ teaspoon cinnamon**
- **¼ teaspoon ground ginger**
- **2 cups couscous (dry precooked semolina cereal)**
- **½ cup dark raisins or currants**
- **½ cup chopped pitted dates**
- **12 ounces zucchini, trimmed and coarsely chopped (about 2 cups)**
- **9 ounces carrots, peeled, trimmed, and coarsely chopped (about 1 cup)**
- **1 large onion, finely chopped**
- **1½ tablespoons freshly squeezed lemon juice, or to taste**
- **½ teaspoon salt, or to taste**
- **1 bunch of kale, washed and dried**
- **½ cup slivered almonds, toasted**

In a large saucepan bring the stock, 4 tablespoons olive oil, turmeric, cinnamon, and ginger to a boil. Add the couscous and boil for 1 to 2 minutes, or until the liquid is absorbed. Remove from the heat and fold in the raisins and dates. Cover tightly and let stand for 15 minutes. Add the zucchini, carrots, and onion; mix well.

In a small bowl combine the lemon juice, remaining 2 tablespoons oil, and salt. Pour over the couscous and toss to coat thoroughly, breaking up any clumps. Cover and refrigerate overnight to blend the flavors.

To serve, bring to room temperature and add more salt and lemon juice, if desired. Arrange the kale decoratively on a large platter, cover with the couscous, and sprinkle with the toasted slivered almonds.

SERVES 8 TO 10

Sesame Cracker Bread

This is the Armenian lavash enriched with butter, and, one could suppose, the original bread made for a host to break with guests. Also very good for nibbling. It freezes well.

> 1   **package active dry yeast**
>   **Pinch of sugar**
> 1   **cup lukewarm water (105° to 115°)**
> 4   **tablespoons (½ stick) unsalted butter, melted**
> 1½ **teaspoons salt**
> 3   **to 3½ cups unbleached all-purpose flour**
> ½   **cup (approximately) sesame seeds**

Dissolve the yeast and sugar in ½ cup lukewarm water. Let sit for 10 minutes, or until the mixture is foamy. In a large mixing bowl, combine the yeast mixture with the remaining ½ cup water, the melted butter, and the salt. Add the flour, 1 cup at a time, blending well, until the dough holds together. Knead on a floured board for 5 to 10 minutes, until smooth and elastic, adding flour as needed. Put the dough in an oiled bowl and turn to coat the entire surface. Cover with a cloth and let rise in a warm draft-free place for 1 hour, until doubled.

Preheat the oven to 350°. Punch down the dough and divide into 24 equal pieces. Cover with a cloth. Spread a few teaspoons of sesame seeds on the board. Remove the dough one piece at a time and roll out on the seeds as thin as possible, into circles about 6 inches in diameter. Be careful not to tear the dough. Add more sesame seeds as needed. If larger crackers are desired, divide the dough into larger pieces.

Bake the crackers on an ungreased baking sheet in the center of the oven for 13 to 15 minutes, until golden brown spots appear. Let cool on racks. Store in an airtight container.

MAKES TWENTY-FOUR 6-INCH CRACKERS

Poached Figs in Port and Custard Sauce

A most appealing dessert, with the fruit coddled in a light custard and enhanced with port.

> 1   **bottle of port (a fifth)**
> 12 **to 16 unpeeled black or green figs, stems left on, slightly ripe**

CUSTARD SAUCE
> 2   **cups milk**
> ½   **vanilla bean, split lengthwise**
> 4   **egg yolks**
> ½   **cup sugar**

GARNISH
> **Sprigs of mint**

In a saucepan, heat the port to a boil and add the figs (make sure that the port covers the figs or poach them in two batches). Reduce the heat and simmer for 15 minutes. With a slotted spoon, remove the figs. Let cool. Increase the heat and reduce the port until syrupy, or until about ¾ cup remains. Set aside while preparing the custard sauce.

Heat the milk slowly with the vanilla bean and bring to a boil. Meanwhile, beat the eggs and sugar together with a whisk or an electric mixer until the mixture runs like a ribbon. Slowly add the hot milk to the egg-sugar mixture. Return the mixture to the pan and cook over medium heat, stirring constantly, until it coats the back of a metal spoon. Remove the vanilla bean. Strain and let cool. Add ¼ cup custard to the port reduction.

To serve, spoon the remaining custard onto individual serving plates. Put 2 figs in the center of each plate and drizzle the port-custard combination over them. Garnish with fresh mint.

SERVES 6 TO 8

Figs garnished with sprigs of fresh mint.

ABALONE BEACH

. . . .

The simplicity of the tea room and its freedom from vulgarity make it truly a sanctuary from the vexations of the outer world," wrote Okakura Kakuzo in *The Book of Tea* in 1906. The artist who built this teahouse on the steep hill below her home in Laguna Beach was not only seeking the sanctuary she had learned to value in Japan, but also may have felt the need to come to terms with the sheer beauty of Laguna, the grandeur of mountains meeting the sea—a collision of the gods.

According to Zen principles, the teahouse is built of seemingly flimsy materials because only the spirit is eternal. The Taoist and Zen philosophies place more stress on the process through which perfection is sought than upon perfection itself. Symmetry is therefore avoided; no color, design, or shape is repeated. Colors are sober, and utensils old. The only decoration is a single painting, with perhaps some flowers. This California teahouse is beautifully located, as it should be, in a tranquil garden overlooking the sea. There is a bridge over a waterfall and a garden path.

The Japanese have been an important influence on both nouvelle and contemporary California cuisine, as can be seen in the meticulous arrangement of dishes and a fascination with undercooking, not to mention no-cooking, as in sushi and sashimi. Californians are fairly passionate about sushi. Knowing the best sushi chef conveys more status than owning a Mercedes.

Sushi can also be made at home, as these recipes show. Perhaps with not quite the same swift grace or precision, but with some pretty little bites resulting. These are versions of nigiri sushi, or *edomae*, Edo being the old name for Tokyo. Rolled in seaweed, they become maki-mono or nori-maki, *nori* being seaweed and *maki* meaning "to cut."

Oriental Lunch

FOR **6**

Chicken Yakitori

Spinach Roll with Sesame Seed Dressing

California Roll

Nori-Maki (with Scallops)

Oriental Oranges

Warm Sake or Gewurztraminer

· · · · · · · · · · ·

Chicken Yakitori

The Japanese, with limited produce, achieve variety by methods of cooking. *Yaki* is broiling or grilling; *tori* is chicken. Yakitori is grilled chicken on a skewer.

- ¾ **cup soy sauce (preferably Japanese)**
- ¾ **cup sake (Japanese rice wine)**
- 1 **tablespoon sugar**
- 1 **small knob of fresh ginger, peeled and squeezed through a garlic press**
- 2 **to 2½ pounds skinless, boneless chicken breasts, cut into 1-inch squares**
- 12 **scallions (white and light green part only), cut into 1-inch pieces**

Prepare a barbecue, hibachi grill, or broiler.

In a medium bowl, combine the soy sauce, sake, sugar, and ginger and stir until the sugar dissolves. Add the chicken and scallions and toss to coat. Marinate for 15 to 30 minutes, turning once or twice.

Alternately thread the chicken and scallions on 6 bamboo skewers (soaked in water) or metal skewers. Reserve the marinade.

Grill or broil 4 to 6 inches from the heat, basting with the marinade and turning once, for 8 to 10 minutes, until the chicken is crisp and cooked through.

SERVES 6

Yakitori is grilled on the hibachi in an airy teahouse. The Japanese jars contain shoyu and sake. A graceful gesture keeps kimono sleeves under control. The yakitori is served in hand-wrought iron bowls (right).

Spinach Roll with Sesame Seed Dressing

Another California innovation, simple to make and a refreshing contrast in both color and taste. Cook the spinach only to a limpness easy to handle.

2   pounds spinach, washed and stems removed
4½ to 5 tablespoons mixed light and dark
     sesame seeds, toasted (see Note below)
1   tablespoon Japanese soy sauce
1   to 2 teaspoons freshly squeezed lemon juice
1   tablespoon mirin (sweet cooking sake)
     or 1 teaspoon sugar

Put the spinach with any water clinging to the leaves in a large frying pan and cook over medium heat, covered, stirring occasionally, for 3 to 4 minutes, just until wilted. Refresh under cold water and let cool. Squeeze out the water with your hands and shape the spinach into a roll about 1 inch in diameter. Roll it in a clean tea towel to remove any excess water.

To make the dressing, mash 1½ to 2 tablespoons sesame seeds with a mortar and pestle. In a small bowl, combine the soy sauce, lemon juice, and mirin. Add the mashed seeds and mix well.

Cut the spinach roll into 6 even pieces and spoon about ½ teaspoon dressing over the top of each piece. Sprinkle with the remaining sesame seeds.

MAKES 6 PIECES

Sushi is eaten with the fingers, in one bite. From the top: scallop nori-maki, spinach roll, California roll, and a garnish of ginger and wasabi on the lower left.

California Roll

Some kindly sushi chef added avocado to nori-maki and called it California. With the crab, it is a logical California taste. Wasabi paste can be mixed with the dipping shoyu (soy sauce), and thinly sliced gari will clear the palate for the next taste. Sushi is eaten with the fingers. In one bite.

2   sheets of toasted nori (dried seaweed),
     approximately 7 inches × 8 inches
1   cup Sushi Rice (page 40)
1   teaspoon powdered wasabi (Japanese
     horseradish) mixed with 1 teaspoon water
¼   avocado, cut lengthwise into thin strips
1   1-inch piece of cucumber, peeled,
     seeded, and cut lengthwise into thin strips
1   teaspoon sesame seeds, toasted (see Note)
2   ounces king crab or surimi crab
     (a combination of various Pacific
     whitefish), shredded or cut lengthwise
     into thin strips, all excess moisture
     squeezed out with paper towels

     Gari (pickled ginger)
     Japanese soy sauce

On a bamboo sushi mat lay a sheet of nori, rough side up, long side at the bottom. Dip your fingers in cold water and pick up a little of the sushi rice at a time, patting it down in a thin layer on the lower half of the nori, all the way to the right and left edges. Spread ½ teaspoon wasabi paste across the rice. Then arrange half of the avocado and cucumber strips lengthwise down the center of the rice. Sprinkle with ½ teaspoon sesame seeds. Lay half the crab end to end across the rice.

Starting at the edge closest to you, roll up the nori tightly, pressing down on the mat to shape the roll; leave a 1-inch margin of nori at the far end. Moisten the end flap with a little water to seal. Remove the roll from the mat and cut (don't saw) it into 8 equal slices about 1 inch thick. Repeat with the remaining nori.

To serve, accompany with gari and a small dish of soy sauce for dipping.

NOTE: Toast sesame seeds in a small frying pan over low heat, stirring constantly. Remove from the heat when the seeds start to make a popping sound.

MAKES 16 PIECES

**Perched on a cliff overlooking the Pacific, the
teahouse offers serenity.**

Nori-Maki (with Scallops)

Nori is seaweed that comes dried and ready to use in Oriental food shops. The trick in making nori-maki is spreading the rice evenly and rolling tightly so it will all hold together.

> ¼ **pound bay scallops, washed and drained**
> **(or sea scallops, cut into small pieces)**
> **Salt**
>
> 2 **sheets of toasted nori (dried seaweed),**
> **approximately 7 inches × 8 inches**
> 1 **cup Sushi Rice (recipe follows)**
> 1 **teaspoon powdered wasabi (Japanese**
> **horseradish) mixed with 1 teaspoon water**
> **Freshly squeezed lemon juice**
> 1 **teaspoon sesame seeds, toasted**
> **(see Note, page 39)**
>
> **Gari (pickled ginger)**
> **Japanese soy sauce**

Line a metal pan with foil and put the scallops in it. Sprinkle with salt. Place under the broiler for 1 minute, until just partially cooked. Remove from the broiler and set aside.

On a bamboo sushi mat, lay out a sheet of nori, rough side up, long side at the bottom. Keeping the work surface dry, dip your fingers in cold water and pick up a little of the sushi rice at a time, patting it down in a thin layer on the lower half of the nori, all the way to the right and left edges. Spread ½ teaspoon wasabi paste across the rice. Arrange half the scallops lengthwise down the center of the rice. Sprinkle with lemon juice and ½ teaspoon sesame seeds.

Starting at the edge closest to you, roll up the nori tightly, pressing down on the mat to shape the roll; leave a 1-inch margin of nori at the far end. Moisten this end flap with a little water to seal. Remove the roll from the mat and cut (don't saw) it into 8 equal slices about 1 inch thick. Repeat with the remaining nori.

To serve, accompany with gari and a small dish of soy sauce for dipping.

MAKES 16 PIECES

. . . .

Sushi Rice

Preparing sushi rice takes a little practice. It must be of a consistency that will hold together without being sticky. Follow the directions exactly and it will all come out fine.

> 1 **cup short-grain rice**
>
> **VINEGAR DRESSING**
> 2 **tablespoons rice vinegar**
> ¾ **tablespoon sugar**
> ½ **to 1 teaspoon salt**

Wash and toss the rice until the water runs clear, and drain in colander for 30 minutes to 1 hour. In a small saucepan with a tight-fitting lid, bring 1¼ cups water to boil, add the rice slowly, and return the water to a full boil. Reduce the heat, cover, and simmer for 10 minutes, until all the water is absorbed. Remove from the heat, take off the lid, spread a clean kitchen towel over the top of the pot, replace the lid, and let stand for 10 to 15 minutes.

Brilliant orange slices, garnished with swirls of candied orange peel, are honorably set forth on a white crackle-glaze plate.

While the rice is cooking, combine the vinegar, sugar, and salt in a small bowl. Stir constantly until the sugar has dissolved. (You can also do this by heating the mixture in a small saucepan. Let cool before using.)

Transfer the rice to a large, shallow, nonmetallic platter and spread it evenly with a large wooden spoon or spatula. Run the wooden spoon through the rice in a right-and-left slicing motion to separate the grains, while at the same time using a uchiwa (fan), a sturdy piece of cardboard, or a hair dryer set on cool to cool the rice. As you do this, slowly pour in the vinegar mixture a little at a time. (You may not need all of it; do not let the rice become mushy.) Continue for about 10 minutes until the rice has cooled to room temperature. (Cooling sushi rice is most easily accomplished with the aid of another person.)

The rice may be prepared a day ahead of time. Cover it tightly, but do not refrigerate.

MAKES ABOUT 2½ CUPS

Oriental Oranges

The Japanese, and also the Chinese, understand the pleasure of a fine orange, perhaps merely quartered, or simply prepared and prettily set forth, as here.

6 large oranges, preferably navel

SYRUP
1 cup sugar
⅓ cup water
   Grenadine (for color)

With a citrus zester carefully remove the peel from the oranges, making sure not to include any of the bitter white pith. (The peel can also be removed with a knife and cut into thin julienne strips.) Cut away the pith from the oranges with a sharp knife. Chill the oranges until serving time.

Blanch the peel in boiling water for 1 to 2 minutes. Repeat three times, using fresh water each time to remove the bitterness.

To make the syrup, bring the sugar, water, and several teaspoons grenadine slowly to a boil, stirring to make sure the sugar is dissolved. Add the orange peel, return to a boil, and cook over low heat for 5 minutes, without stirring. With a slotted spoon, transfer the peel to a plate covered with wax paper, cover, and set aside until just before serving time. Reserve the syrup.

To serve, slice the oranges, overlap slices on individual dishes, and spoon the syrup over them. Arrange the candied peel on top.

The oranges, syrup, and candied peel can all be prepared ahead of time, but do not assemble until just before serving.

SERVES 6

SANTA BARBARA

No one who lives in Santa Barbara wants to leave, and everyone who visits wants to stay. Ninety miles north of Los Angeles, the air is crisp, the weather gentle, and walking more practical than driving. Cradled by what Richard Henry Dana (*Two Years Before the Mast*) called its "amphitheater of mountains," and calmed by the ocean, it is a small dream city kept alert by big-city amenities.

History—and a landmark—is preserved in the well-kept dignity of one of the finer missions. There is decent theater, a major music festival a few miles away in Ojai, a first-class art museum—and everywhere craftsmen display their wares.

With Julia Child now in part-time residence, the contented Santa Barbarans are being nudged into considering the finer points of contemporary cooking. The American Institute of Wine and Food will be headquartered at the Santa Barbara campus of the University of California in the near future, and some fine chefs work diligently at leading the natives into gastronomic temptation. There are wild mushrooms in the mountains, local produce is of high quality, and the Santa Barbara prawn was one of the great discoveries of the last few years.

Supper was served on the porch of a home in Carpinteria, on the southern edge of the city, overlooking the ocean and lonesome, rolling sand dunes. It was so quiet, seemingly so remote, that civilization might never have happened—except to build a house and prepare the dinner.

The meal is simple but, as always in this style of cooking, with an alerting challenge to the tastebuds: orange in the tomato soup and basil in the zucchini to balance the down-home taste of corn cakes, and the exotic flavor of cassis in the ice cream.

TWILIGHT BARBECUE

FOR **8**

Fresh Tomato Soup with Orange

Grilled Swordfish with Anchovy-Caper Butter

Julienne of Zucchini with Pistachio Pesto

Corn Cakes

Cassis Ice Cream with Mixed Berries

Pinot Chardonnay

. . . .

On those occasions when wine is not desired, civilized substitutes would include bottled waters, fresh fruit juices, or what are being called coolers. A cooler can be almost anything—one or several fruit juices blended with ice cream, or eggs, or sparkling water, or wine (nonalcoholic if preferred). Vegetable juices spiked with herbs are refreshing too—tomato with basil, cucumber with dill, etc. Non-grape wines—made of peaches, pears, or berries—also make wonderful coolers. So does tea, by itself or with fruit juices.

Waters generally come from natural springs, with distinctive differences in taste, and without calories or salt. Some have added natural fruit flavors, mostly lemon, lime, and orange, some cherry, and at least one cola berry.

All these should be served in tall frosty glasses, filled with ice and garnished with whole berries, slices of fruit, sticks of vegetables, sprigs of herbs, etc.

A combination of fruit juices over ice (top right). Natural spring water with lime slices (top far right). Strawberry wine and sparkling water (bottom right).

Fresh Tomato Soup with Orange

A most refreshing soup, best made with red ripe tomatoes; however, good imported canned Italian plum tomatoes can be substituted.

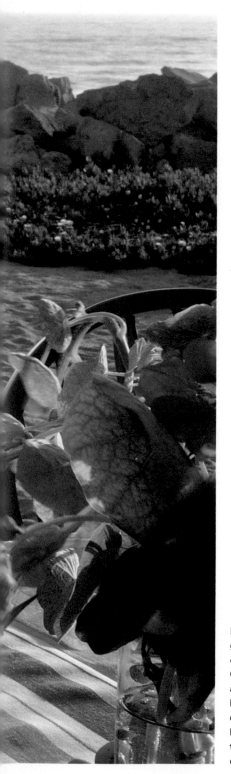

Fresh tomato soup garnished with twists of orange peel (above). Grilled swordfish, zucchini, and corn cakes on a hand-painted French earthenware plate (left). Nasturtiums cut from the garden were the centerpiece.

4 pounds fresh ripe tomatoes, peeled, halved, and seeded, or 2 cans of plum tomatoes (1 pound 12 ounces each), drained and seeded
2 medium onions, peeled and sliced
2 medium carrots, peeled and sliced
4 tablespoons (½ stick) unsalted butter
6 to 7 cups chicken or veal stock, preferably homemade (page 17 or page 169)
1 large bay leaf
1 strip of lemon peel, about ½ inch × 3 inches
2 tablespoons unbleached all-purpose flour
½ cup freshly squeezed orange juice
½ teaspoon sugar
1 teaspoon salt
Freshly ground white pepper, to taste
Sour cream

GARNISH
Orange peel twists or grated rind

Simmer the tomatoes, stirring occasionally, in a shallow uncovered pan over medium heat for about 30 minutes. Set aside. In a large saucepan, sauté the onions and carrots in 2 tablespoons butter, stirring, for 10 minutes, until soft. Add the tomatoes, stock, bay leaf, and lemon peel. Cook for 10 minutes. Remove the bay leaf and lemon peel and purée the mixture until smooth in a food processor fitted with the steel blade. Strain through a sieve, if desired.

In a large clean saucepan melt the remaining 2 tablespoons butter and whisk in the flour. Cook for 1 to 2 minutes, then add the soup mixture and bring to a boil, stirring constantly. Reduce the heat and simmer for 10 minutes. Add the orange juice, sugar, salt, and pepper. Adjust the seasonings if necessary. Serve immediately, with a dollop of sour cream. Garnish with a twist of orange peel or grated orange rind.

SERVES 8

An inspired combination of flavors and textures.

Prepare a barbecue and brush the grill with oil. Grill the swordfish 4 to 6 inches above the coals, turning once, and brushing often with melted butter, until the fish tests done. This will take about 6 to 8 minutes if the fish is ¾ inch thick, about 10 to 15 minutes if it is 1 inch thick.

Just before the fish is ready, cut the anchovy-caper butter into 8 equal slices. Remove the fish from the grill and put a pat of the butter on each swordfish steak. Serve immediately.

SERVES 8

. . . .

Julienne of Zucchini with Pistachio Pesto

A splendid treatment for zucchini, or any of the summer squashes. Instead of a mandoline, an ordinary grater will do. Pistachios add another flavor to the usual pine nuts of pesto.

- ¼ **cup shelled pistachio nuts**
- ⅓ **cup pine nuts**
- 3 **medium garlic cloves (or substitute 2 large shallots, minced, for a more delicate flavor)**
- 1 **cup firmly packed fresh basil leaves**
- ½ **to ¾ cup extra virgin olive oil**
- ¼ **to ½ teaspoon salt**
- 5 **to 6 tablespoons unsalted butter**
- 2½ **to 3 pounds zucchini, cut into matchstick-size julienne (preferably on a mandoline)**

Parboil the pistachio nuts for 2 minutes, then rub briskly between towels to remove the skins. Put the pistachios, pine nuts, and garlic in the bowl of a food processor fitted with the steel blade. Process to a fine paste. Add the basil and process until puréed. With the machine running, add enough olive oil in a thin stream to make a mayonnaise consistency. Add salt to taste and set aside (see Note).

Sauté the zucchini in butter for 4 to 5 minutes, until crisp-tender. Add the pesto and quickly toss to heat through. Serve immediately.

NOTE: The pesto may be made ahead and refrigerated or frozen. Before using, bring to room temperature.

SERVES 8

Grilled Swordfish with Anchovy-Caper Butter

The swordfish was beloved in Southern California long before contemporary cooks added their refinements. Its firm texture makes it a natural for the barbecue, and the anchovy-caper butter is contemporary imagination.

- 8 **tablespoons (1 stick) unsalted butter, at room temperature**
- 4 **teaspoons minced capers**
- 2 **teaspoons freshly squeezed and strained lemon juice**
- 1 **large garlic clove, crushed**
- 3 **anchovy fillets, rinsed, dried, and mashed**
- 8 **swordfish steaks, ¾ to 1 inch thick Unsalted butter, melted**

Cream the butter with the capers, lemon juice, and garlic. Press the anchovies through a fine sieve and add to the butter mixture. Combine well. Using a piece of plastic wrap to aid you, roll the butter mixture into a log. Close tightly and refrigerate for at least 1 hour.

Corn Cakes

Not as difficult as the delicate corn fritter, but with a similar effect from the flavor and texture of fresh corn kernels.

1¾ cups unbleached all-purpose flour
¼ cup yellow cornmeal
2 teaspoons baking powder
2 teaspoons sugar
1 teaspoon salt
3 eggs, lightly beaten
2 cups milk
4 tablespoons (½ stick) unsalted butter, melted
¼ cup vegetable oil
2 cups fresh corn kernels (cut from 3 to 4 ears of corn)

Sift together the flour, cornmeal, baking powder, sugar, and salt. Make a well in the center and add the eggs and milk. Stir until blended. Add the melted butter and vegetable oil and mix again. Fold in the corn very gently; do not overmix.

Heat and grease a griddle or skillet. Pour out enough batter to make 4-inch pancakes. When bubbles form, turn and brown the other side. Keep finished pancakes warm in a low oven. Serve immediately.

MAKES SIXTEEN TO TWENTY 4-INCH PANCAKES

The simple elegance of ice cream and perfectly ripe berries in a French earthenware bowl.

Cassis Ice Cream with Mixed Berries

Pretty desserts are a must in California cooking, and nothing could be prettier than this medley of bright berries with mauve-colored ice cream.

4 cups half-and-half
½ cup sugar (preferably superfine)
¾ tablespoon vanilla extract
¾ cup crème de cassis
1 cup black currant or blackberry preserves, strained through a sieve

Mixed berries, such as red or golden raspberries, blueberries, and blackberries

Stir the sugar into the half-and-half until the sugar dissolves. Add the vanilla, crème de cassis, and preserves. Freeze in an ice-cream machine according to the manufacturer's directions.

Serve with a mixture of fresh berries.

MAKES APPROXIMATELY 1½ QUARTS

HARBOR ISLAND

There are marinas all along the California coast, but somehow boats seem to belong more naturally to Balboa Bay than to other newer, shinier places. Newport Beach and its cheek-by-jowl neighbor, Balboa, are seafaring towns, complete with canals, channels, and five islands: Harbor, Lido, Linda, Bay, and Balboa, lined with elegant homes and yachts.

Everyone here seems to have a boat; if not, his neighbor does. More than nine thousand boats of all sizes are anchored along the bayfront. Some travel to Catalina, Mexico, and Hawaii, some sail on until West becomes East—and they all cruise the bay for cocktails at sunset.

A cocktail buffet was served aboard a new, ultra-modern yacht. Dinner was served on a more traditional but equally luxurious working yacht just back from Alaska, with a huge refrigerated hold filled with the owner's catch.

Although both of these yachts have large kitchens with sufficient space to prepare even the most complicated menus, most boat owners are not so blessed, and for them, the secret of entertaining aboard is doing everything possible in a kitchen that is not a galley. For the cocktail buffet, the basic preparation of the hors d'oeuvres could almost all be done ahead, needing only the final assembling on board. The raw vegetables could be pared and cut to nicely sized sticks, the asparagus briefly blanched, and carried on ice. The melon and pineapple could be peeled and cut to manageable size. (The slivered fresh ginger here is a nice touch.) Strawberries require only a rinse and a check for blemishes.

The dinner could come aboard with salmon ready for the oven, cucumbers needing only the last step, one sauce to be finished, the other to be warmed.

Cocktail Buffet

FOR 12

Crudités of Jicama, Asparagus, and Mixed Bell Peppers

Smoked Salmon in Cucumber Cups

Herbed Brie and Walnut Tart • Spiced Pecans

Steak Tartare on Pumpernickel • Mustard-Dill Shrimp

Melon and Pineapple with Ginger

Strawberries with Sour Cream and Brown Sugar

Blanc de Noir or Brut Sparkling

. . . .

Assorted hors d'oeuvres and spiced pecans.

Appetizers cut into interesting shapes. Crudités, fresh fruit, and spiced pecans are elegantly arranged on modern trays of silver and glass. The black-and-white wine holders, shaped like a ship's smokestack, perfectly fit the setting.

Smoked Salmon in Cucumber Cups

There are many ways of curing salmon, of which smoking is only one. Taste different kinds to find your favorite.

    6 ounces cream cheese, at room temperature
    ¾ cup crème fraîche (see Note)
    3 seedless cucumbers
    4 to 6 ounces smoked salmon
    1 bunch of chives

Combine the cream cheese and crème fraîche in an electric mixer. Refrigerate until the mixture is firm.

Wash and dry the cucumbers, and cut each into 5 equal pieces. Then cut each piece diagonally across the center so that it has a flat bottom and slanted top and measures about 1½ inches wide. There should be 30 pieces. With a small melon baller, scoop out a hole in each diagonally cut side, being careful not to cut completely through the cucumber. Fill each cup with some of the cream cheese mixture. Roll up a third or a half slice of smoked salmon and insert decoratively. Garnish with 1 or 2 fresh chives.

VARIATION: Slice celery stalks horizontally at a 10° to 20° angle to form chevrons. Place a dollop of the cream cheese mixture in the center. Top with salmon roe.

NOTE: Crème fraîche is available in gourmet shops and some supermarkets. To make it at home, combine 1 cup heavy cream with 2 teaspoons buttermilk or ½ cup sour cream and stir over very low heat until lukewarm. Pour into a clean bowl, cover lightly, and let sit at room temperature until thickened. This may take several hours or overnight. Refrigerate for up to 1 week.

MAKES 30 CUCUMBER CUPS

Brie tart, sliced for easy handling, is edged by
cucumber chevrons topped with salmon roe.

Herbed Brie and Walnut Tart

Brie is a marvelous cheese, but difficult to manage
at a cocktail party, where everyone needs three hands
anyway. Putting it in a crust solves the problem. The
good Brie flavor will be there without the runniness.

PASTRY CRUST

1¾ cups pastry flour or unbleached all-
purpose flour

½ teaspoon salt

8 tablespoons (1 stick) unsalted butter,
well chilled, cut into 16 equal pieces

¼ cup solid vegetable shortening, well
chilled, cut into small pieces

4 to 5 tablespoons ice water

FILLING

14 ounces Brie, well chilled

14 ounces cream cheese, at room temperature

3 eggs

¾ cup chopped walnuts (plus more for the
top, if desired)

1 teaspoon finely ground dried rosemary
Salt and freshly ground white pepper, to taste

GARNISH

Fresh rosemary

To make the crust, put the flour, salt, and butter in the
bowl of a food processor fitted with the steel blade and
pulse 10 times. Add the shortening and pulse 10 more
times. With the machine running, pour in 4 tablespoons of ice water through the feed tube and immediately turn the machine off. Transfer the contents to a
flat work surface and quickly form the dough into a
round. If the dough is too dry, add the additional tablespoon of ice water drop by drop. Flatten the dough
into a disk, wrap in plastic wrap, and refrigerate for 1
hour or more.

Roll out the dough and use it to line a 12-inch tart pan
with a removable bottom. Prick the bottom with a
fork. Freeze for 1 hour.

Preheat the oven to 375°. Remove the pan from the
freezer, line it with aluminum foil, fill with pie
weights or beans, and bake for 30 to 40 minutes (removing the foil and weights halfway through the baking time), until golden brown. Let cool.

To make the filling, remove the crust from the Brie
with a sharp knife moistened with water. Bring the
Brie to room temperature. Combine well with the
cream cheese in a mixer. Add the eggs, one at a time,
and blend well. Stir in the walnuts, dried rosemary,
salt, and pepper.

Preheat the oven to 300°. Fill the chilled pastry shell
with the cheese mixture, sprinkle with additional walnuts if desired, and bake for 30 to 40 minutes. Cover
loosely with foil if the nuts become too brown. Serve
warm or at room temperature, garnished with fresh
rosemary and cut into thin wedges.

MAKES ONE 12-INCH TART

. . . .

Spiced Pecans

A tempting variation on the Hunan treatment of
walnuts. They are easy to prepare, but be careful not to
let them burn. Make lots; these are nice to give as gifts.

3 tablespoons unsalted butter, melted

¼ teaspoon cayenne pepper

½ teaspoon cinnamon

2 teaspoons salt

3 tablespoons Worcestershire sauce

3 to 4 drops Tabasco sauce

4 cups (1 pound) whole pecans

Preheat the oven to 300°. Combine the melted butter
with all the seasonings. Add the pecans and toss well.
Spread on a large ungreased baking sheet and bake for
10 minutes. Remove to stir and toss the pecans with a
spatula so they will bake evenly. Return to the oven for
5 to 10 minutes longer, until the pecans have dried
slightly. Let cool and store in an airtight container.
The pecans may be frozen.

MAKES 4 CUPS

Steak Tartare on Pumpernickel

Steak tartare can also be attractively mounded on a platter with its garnishes so guests can spread their own.

- 1 **pound lean top round or top sirloin of beef, freshly ground twice (see Note)**
- 3 **anchovy fillets, finely minced**
- ½ **medium onion, finely minced**
- 1 **teaspoon Dijon-style mustard**
- 2 **egg yolks**
- 1 **tablespoon minced fresh parsley**
- 1½ **teaspoons snipped chives**
- 2 **tablespoons Cognac or brandy**
- 1 **teaspoon salt**
- ½ **teaspoon freshly ground black pepper**
  Dash of Worcestershire sauce (optional)
- 1 **loaf thinly sliced pumpernickel bread, crusts removed**

GARNISH
Chopped hard-cooked egg
Grated fresh horseradish
Capers
Chopped red onion

Put the meat on a cutting board. Make a well in the center and add the anchovies, onion, mustard, egg yolks, parsley, chives, Cognac or brandy, salt, pepper, and Worcestershire sauce, if desired. With the dull side of two heavy-bladed knives, blend the mixture well, chopping it to flatten the mound and then scraping it back into a mound. Add more mustard, salt, or pepper if necessary.

Spread the mixture on the bread slices and cut each slice into 6 or 8 rectangles. Transfer to a serving plate. If desired, garnish with chopped hard-cooked egg, grated horseradish, capers, and/or chopped red onion.

NOTE: Be sure to use *very* fresh beef and prepare the dish on the day it is to be served. The meat is superior ground in a meat grinder (your butcher should do it for you), but if you wish to do it yourself, cut it into 1-inch chunks and freeze. Remove from the freezer, defrost until the tip of a knife will pierce the meat, then, using on-and-off pulses, coarsely chop in a food processor fitted with the steel blade.

SERVES 12 OR MORE

A still-life of shrimp, cucumber cups, and steak tartare.

Mustard-Dill Shrimp

This is a tasty variation on a Scandinavian open-faced sandwich. Made in a larger size, it would be nice for lunch.

- 1 **pound raw medium-size shrimp (approximately 30 shrimp), peeled and deveined (or 1 pound cooked bay shrimp)**

MUSTARD-DILL DRESSING
- 2 **tablespoons Dijon-style mustard**
- 1 **tablespoon sugar, or to taste**
- 1½ **tablespoons white wine vinegar**
- ¼ **teaspoon salt**
- 2 **tablespoons finely chopped fresh dill or 2 teaspoons dried**
- ⅔ **cup vegetable oil**

- 7 **to 8 slices of Limpa Bread (page 176) or other firm-textured bread**
  Unsalted butter, at room temperature
- 1 **to 2 heads of Boston lettuce, best leaves only**

GARNISH
Zest of 2 to 3 lemons
Fresh dill or parsley

Drop the fresh shrimp into a pot of salted boiling water. Reduce the heat at once and simmer for about 2 minutes, just until the shrimp turn pink. Do not overcook. Drain at once.

To make the dressing, combine all the ingredients except the oil in a food processor fitted with the steel blade. Slowly pour in the oil, and process until the dressing is emulsified.

In a bowl, gently mix the cooked shrimp and enough dressing to coat. Refrigerate.

With a cookie cutter, cut each slice of bread into 4 rounds. Butter each round, and cover with a small piece of lettuce. Top with a shrimp and garnish with lemon zest and a sprig of dill or parsley. Serve at once.

MAKES ABOUT 30 PIECES

DINNER AT SUNSET

FOR **6**

Crab Claws with Lime-Cilantro Cocktail Sauce

Pacific Salmon with Two Sauces

Tarragon Cucumbers

Endive and Watercress Salad with Baked Goat Cheese

Tangerine Ice

Brut Sparkling

. . . .

Dungeness crab.

Crab Claws with Lime-Cilantro Cocktail Sauce

Crab claws were hors d'oeuvres in the launch taking guests to the yacht. If in season, fresh Dungeness crab legs would be good, too.

24 **frozen snow crab claws, or
     6 Dungeness crab legs**

LIME-CILANTRO COCKTAIL SAUCE
1 **cup ketchup**
2 **tablespoons white horseradish, freshly
    grated or bottled
    Juice of 1 lime**
2 **tablespoons chopped fresh cilantro**

Defrost frozen crab claws overnight in the refrigerator or for 2 to 3 hours at room temperature.

Combine the ketchup, horseradish, lime juice, and cilantro and chill thoroughly.

Serve the crab claws, thoroughly chilled, on a bed of chopped ice, accompanied by a bowl of the sauce for dipping.

SERVES 6

Aboard the launch, sparkling wine and chilled crab claws with their dipping sauce are ready to serve as a prelude to dinner.

Miniature roses in a small silver bowl echo the color of the salmon.

Pacific Salmon with Two Sauces

Of the five species of Pacific salmon, Chinook is considered the finest. This pretty dish was inspired by a recipe created by French chef Georges Le Blanc.

  2 pounds salmon fillets with skin
    Salt

MUSTARD CREAM SAUCE
  1 cup crème fraîche (see Note, page 53)
  1 tablespoon grainy French mustard
    (Moutarde de Meaux)

TOMATO BUTTER SAUCE
  3 tablespoons olive oil
2½ pounds ripe tomatoes, peeled, seeded, and finely diced
  1 tablespoon minced fresh thyme or 1 teaspoon dried
    Salt and freshly ground black pepper, to taste
  3 tablespoons dry white wine
  3 tablespoons white wine vinegar
1½ tablespoons finely chopped shallots
  ¼ cup crème fraîche (see Note, page 53)
  6 tablespoons (¾ stick) unsalted butter, cut into small pieces

Lay the salmon on a cutting board, skin side down. With a long, thin, flexible knife, cut at a 30° angle into ½-inch thick slices. Discard the skin. Put the salmon on a well-greased heavy baking sheet and sprinkle lightly with salt. Refrigerate until ready to bake.

To make the mustard cream sauce, combine the crème fraîche with the mustard and set aside.

To make the tomato butter sauce, heat the olive oil in a medium skillet and sauté the tomatoes over moderately high heat, stirring, for about 7 minutes, until thick and well reduced. Add the thyme, salt, and pepper. Remove from the heat and set aside.

Put the wine, wine vinegar, and shallots into a nonaluminum saucepan and, over medium high heat, boil until almost all of the liquid is evaporated. Whisk in the crème fraîche and quickly reduce by half. Add the butter, a piece at a time, whisking constantly. When the mixture is a thick foamy sauce, combine with the reserved tomatoes. Adjust the seasonings and keep warm.

Preheat the oven to 500°. Remove the salmon from the refrigerator and bake for 4 minutes. Meanwhile, warm the mustard cream in a saucepan. To serve, spoon the tomato butter sauce onto 6 warm dinner plates. Put 2 slices of salmon on top of the sauce and spoon the mustard cream over the salmon. Serve immediately.

SERVES 6

Tarragon Cucumbers

Cucumbers are a natural with seafood, as Scandinavians have known for a long time. This method preserves their fresh crispness, and tarragon is a fine complement.

- 1½ pounds (about 3 medium) cucumbers, unpeeled (see Note)
- 3 tablespoons unsalted butter
- ½ teaspoon salt
  Freshly ground white pepper to taste
- 1 tablespoon chopped fresh tarragon

Using a citrus zester or the tines of a fork, make striations down the length of the cucumbers. Cut each in half lengthwise, and with a melon baller or a spoon, scoop out the seeds. Cut each half crosswise into slices ¼ to ⅜ inch thick. Drop the slices into salted boiling water and cook for 1 to 2 minutes, just until crisp-tender. Drain and immediately plunge into cold water to stop the cooking. Drain again and set aside.

Melt the butter in a skillet. Add the cucumbers and salt and pepper. Sauté over medium heat for 2 to 3 minutes, until tender. Add the tarragon, stir to combine, and serve immediately.

N O T E : Seedless cucumbers may also be used; however, the color will be less vivid and the flavor different.

SERVES 6

Chèvre with endive and watercress.

Endive and Watercress Salad with Baked Goat Cheese

Goat cheese with strong-flavored greens is a hallmark of California cooking. Radicchio, arugula, and/or mâche (lamb's lettuce) could be substituted for the endive and watercress.

- 12 1-inch-thick rounds of California chèvre or other fresh mild goat cheese
- 1 cup extra virgin olive oil
- 2 small garlic cloves, minced
- ½ teaspoon freshly ground black pepper
- 10 to 12 fresh basil leaves, torn into pieces
- 2 teaspoons fresh rosemary
- 1 cup fine dry bread crumbs

DRESSING
  MAKES ABOUT 2 CUPS
- 2 teaspoons Dijon-style mustard
- ¼ cup sherry or red wine vinegar
- 2 egg yolks
- 1 cup safflower oil, plus reserved oil from the goat cheese marinade
  Salt and freshly ground black pepper, to taste

- 2 bunches of watercress, tough ends removed
- 3 large compact heads of Belgian endive, leaves separated

Put the cheese in a shallow dish. Combine the oil, garlic, pepper, basil, and rosemary. Pour over the cheese. Turn the cheese to coat all sides. Let sit for a minimum of 1 hour. Baste with the oil several times.

Preheat the oven to 450°. Remove the cheese from the oil, reserving the oil for the dressing. Coat the cheese with bread crumbs and place on a baking sheet.

To make the dressing, combine the mustard, vinegar, and egg yolks in a small bowl. Whisk to blend thoroughly. Slowly add the safflower oil, then the reserved olive oil, whisking constantly. (Do not use a food processor or the dressing will be too thick.) Add salt and pepper.

Bake the cheese for 6 to 10 minutes, until it begins to bubble. Toss the watercress and endive with enough dressing to coat, and arrange on individual salad plates. Put 2 slices of warm cheese on each plate and serve immediately.

SERVES 6

Threads of candied citrus garnish this ice.

Tangerine Ice

Tangerine ice is tart, cool, and pretty, with the flavor emphasized by candied citrus peel.

3½ **cups tangerine juice (preferably freshly squeezed from honey tangerines)**
¾ **cup sugar**
1 **to 2 tablespoons freshly squeezed and strained lemon juice**

GARNISH
Candied Citrus Peel (recipe follows)

In a medium saucepan, mix together the tangerine juice, sugar, and lemon juice. Cook the mixture over low heat for about 5 minutes, stirring to dissolve the sugar. Let cool to room temperature, then chill for at least 1 hour.

Freeze the mixture in an ice-cream machine according to the manufacturer's directions. Transfer to a plastic container and refreeze until serving time.

If you do not have an ice-cream freezer, put the tangerine mixture in a shallow metal pan and freeze until solid (at least 2 or 3 hours). Break up the mixture into several pieces, transfer to a food processor fitted with the steel blade, and, using on-and-off pulses, process until smooth. Return to the shallow pan and refreeze.

Let the ice stand at room temperature for about 10 minutes before serving. Scoop into individual goblets or serving dishes and garnish with strips of candied citrus peel, if desired.

SERVES 6

. . . .

Candied Citrus Peel

These pretty little sweets keep indefinitely in the refrigerator, handy for garnishing all sorts of things —fruit, ice cream, pudding, etc. Cut into larger strips, they make a fine after-dinner nibble. Dip one end in chocolate for a bit of elegance.

3 **oranges or lemons, or a combination of these**
1 **cup sugar**
¼ **cup water**
1 **teaspoon light corn syrup**

With a vegetable peeler or very sharp paring knife, remove strips of peel from the citrus, making sure that no white pith is included. With a sharp knife, cut the strips into fine julienne.

Put the peel in a saucepan, cover with cold water, and bring to a boil. Reduce the heat and simmer for 10 to 15 minutes. Drain and rinse under cold water.

In a medium saucepan combine the sugar, water, and corn syrup. Place over low heat and stir until the sugar is dissolved and the liquid is clear. Cover and continue cooking until the syrup registers 238° on a candy thermometer. Drop in the peel and boil slowly until the mixture thickens, which should take several minutes. Let cool completely. Refrigerate in the liquid in a covered jar.

Guests are ferried in a launch to the yacht anchored in the deeper waters of the bay.

Dinner at Sunset **61**

CARMEL/MONTEREY

It has been said by the myth makers that when the continent of Pacifica sank into the sea, a piece broke off and became the Monterey Peninsula. The gods could not bear to destroy such beauty. If we skip the Mission period, the first white settlers in Carmel were artists, writers, and musicians, sensitive souls who protected their heritage with laws that still forbid neon signs, high-rises, and house numbers. In Carmel, roads divide and go around the trees, and mail is picked up at the post office. Only outlanders find this eccentric.

This is Ansel Adams country, immediately familiar from his photographic understanding of the many moods of the sea. "The one common note of all this country," wrote Robert Louis Stevenson, "is the haunting presence of the ocean.... Everywhere, even in quiet weather, the low, distant, thrilling roar of the Pacific hangs over the coast and the adjacent country like smoke above the battle."

Lunch was on the deck of a home overlooking a lonesome beach of rolling dunes strewn with driftwood and great boulders. Just below the house was a field of artichokes. California produces the entire commerical crop in the United States, and Castroville, a few miles inland, bills itself as the artichoke center of the world. This was to be a lunch of the region, with artichoke soup and a shortcake made with the particularly fine strawberries of the Carmel Valley.

There was a picnic on another day along 17-Mile Drive, one of the most spectacular roads of the world. The marvelously twisted Monterey cypress grows only in this area, and never more than 350 feet from the sea. Once a year, classic cars parade along the Drive in a Grand Concourse. Our picnickers arrived in a vintage Bentley, attired in dusters, veils, and flowing scarves. It was a formal picnic of the period—updated.

OUTDOOR LUNCH

FOR **4**

Fresh Artichoke Soup

Papaya and Avocado Salad with Marinated Prawns

Hard Rolls

Strawberry Shortcake with Sour Cream

Emerald Riesling or Chenin Blanc

. . . .

The California poppy.

Artichoke soup is a fitting start for this lunch of the region.

Fresh Artichoke Soup

A very pretty soup, subtle in color and flavor.

- 2 medium artichokes
- 1 quart chicken stock, preferably homemade (page 17)
- 1 cup beef stock, preferably homemade (page 218)
- 1 cup water
- ¼ cup dry white wine
- 1 small boiling potato, peeled and cubed
- ¼ cup chopped onion
- 3 celery stalks, thinly sliced
- 1 small turnip, peeled and cubed
- 1 small leek (white part only), thinly sliced
- ¼ cup chopped fresh parsley
- 1 tablespoon freshly squeezed lemon juice
- ¼ teaspoon dried oregano
- ¼ teaspoon dried marjoram
- ¼ teaspoon ground coriander
- ¼ teaspoon dried thyme
- Salt and freshly ground black pepper, to taste
- ¼ cup heavy cream

GARNISH
Additional cooked artichoke hearts,
chopped, and tender inside leaves

Cut off the stem and pointed top of each artichoke. Trim the prickly points with a scissors and snap off the tough bottom leaves. Quarter the artichokes, remove and discard the chokes, and remove the inner leaves, reserving some for garnishing.

Combine all remaining ingredients except the cream in a large enamel or stainless steel saucepan, add the artichoke quarters, and bring to a boil. Let simmer, covered, for 2 hours. Purée the solids with a small amount of the liquid in a food processor fitted with the steel blade. Strain the purée through a medium sieve and return it to the soup. Add the cream. Mix well and correct the seasonings. Heat through before serving but do not let boil. Garnish with chopped cooked artichoke hearts, and decorate with the reserved leaves, if desired.

SERVES 4

Papaya and Avocado Salad with Marinated Prawns

The avocado is a native of Mexico that thrives in Southern California. It is often found in a California meal, comfortable with almost anything—papaya and prawns, for instance.

COURT BOUILLON
- 2 cups dry white wine
- 8 cups water
- 4 sprigs of parsley
- Juice of 4 lemons
- 3 large bay leaves

- 16 prawns or large shrimp, peeled and deveined, tails left on
- ¼ cup extra virgin olive oil
- ¼ cup dry white wine
- 2 teaspoons freshly squeezed lemon juice
- 2 tablespoons chopped onion

HONEY LIME DRESSING
- 2 shallots, chopped
- 2 tablespoons honey
- ¼ cup freshly squeezed lime juice
- ⅔ cup extra virgin olive oil

- 2 ripe papayas
- 2 ripe avocados
- 1 small cucumber
- 2 heads of Belgian endive
- 1 small head of red leaf lettuce
- 1 small head of Boston lettuce
- 1 bunch of spinach, stems removed
- ¼ cup toasted walnuts, chopped

GARNISH
Sprigs of watercress
Nasturtium flowers

To prepare the court bouillon, combine all the ingredients in a large pot and bring to a boil. Reduce the heat and let simmer for 1 hour.

Add the prawns to the simmering liquid and poach for about 3 minutes, just until they turn pink and become firm. Do not overcook. Remove with a slotted spoon and rinse under cold water to stop the cooking.

Combine the olive oil, wine, lemon juice, and onion in a bowl. Marinate the prawns in this mixture for approximately 2 hours, turning once or twice.

To make the dressing, combine all the ingredients in a food processor fitted with the steel blade and process until well combined.

Cut the papayas in half and discard the seeds. Peel and slice lengthwise into ½-inch-wide wedges. Cut the avocados in half, remove the pits, peel, and slice lengthwise into ½-inch-wide wedges. Peel the cucumber and slice thinly on the diagonal.

On each serving plate prepare a bed of the endive, red leaf lettuce, Boston lettuce, and spinach, using only the best leaves. If you like, tear some of the leaves into smaller pieces. With a slotted spoon remove the prawns from the marinade and arrange on top of the greens along with the papaya, avocado, and cucumber. Sprinkle with the walnuts and drizzle on the dressing. Garnish with watercress and nasturtiums, if desired.

SERVES 4 AS A MAIN COURSE

A sprightly prawn salad sprinkled with walnuts and garnished with nasturtiums.

Strawberry Shortcake with Sour Cream

Californians cannot claim the strawberry, although perhaps we grow them bigger than anywhere else. Save a few beauties for garnishing this shortcake, which is close to the one our grandmothers used to make.

SHORTCAKE
- **2 cups sifted unbleached all-purpose flour**
- **1 tablespoon baking powder**
- **¾ teaspoon salt**
- **¼ cup sugar**
- **3 ounces cream cheese, cut into pieces**
- **2 tablespoons unsalted butter, cut into pieces**
- **1 egg, beaten**
- **½ cup milk (approximately)**
- **Unsalted butter, melted**

TOPPING
- **2 pints fresh strawberries**
- **¼ cup sugar**
- **2 cups sour cream**
- **Sifted confectioners' sugar, to taste**

Preheat the oven to 425°. Grease a baking sheet and set aside. Sift together the flour, baking powder, salt, and sugar. Cut in the cream cheese and butter with a pastry blender or two knives until the mixture resembles coarse meal.

Pour the beaten egg into a measuring cup and add enough milk to make ¾ cup. Stir the egg-milk mixture slowly into the flour mixture. Knead on a lightly floured surface for about 20 seconds. Divide the dough in half and roll out each piece approximately ¼ inch thick. With a biscuit cutter, cut six 3- to 4-inch rounds from each piece, for a total of twelve rounds. Put six rounds on the baking sheet, brush with melted butter, and top with the remaining rounds. Bake for 12 to 15 minutes, until golden. Remove to a cooling rack.

Wash, hull, and slice the strawberries. Add ¼ cup sugar, or more to taste, and let stand for 10 minutes. Sweeten the sour cream with confectioners' sugar. To serve, split the shortcakes and place the bottom halves on individual plates. Top with some of the sour cream and strawberries. Place the upper halves on top, and cover with the remaining berries and sour cream.

SERVES 6

An almost old-fashioned shortcake.

GRAND CONCOURSE PICNIC

FOR **6**

Meat Terrine with Tomatoes

Eggplant Caviar

Snow Pea, Yellow Bell Pepper, and Mushroom Salad

Pita Herb Triangles

Lemon Tart with Grand Marnier Cream

Brut Sparkling or Gamay

. . . .

The feast is spread on a red and white cotton blanket and served on old stoneware. An antique pitcher holds stock, lilac, and daisies.

Meat Terrine with Tomatoes

A hearty country dish convenient for picnics, very close to an old-fashioned meat loaf, but modernized with porcini mushrooms—the beloved Italian relative of the cèpe.

- 1 ¾-ounce package dried porcini mushrooms
- 1 cup lukewarm water
- 2 tablespoons unsalted butter
- 2 tablespoons finely chopped shallots
- 2 tablespoons finely chopped onion
- ½ teaspoon finely minced garlic
- 2 to 3 Italian plum tomatoes, peeled, seeded, and chopped (or substitute ½ cup canned tomatoes, drained, seeded, and chopped)
- Salt and freshly ground black pepper, to taste
- 1 pound ground lean beef
- 1 pound ground lean pork
- ¼ pound chicken livers, finely diced
- 1 cup fresh bread crumbs
- 2 eggs, lightly beaten
- 3 tablespoons finely minced fresh parsley

Reconstitute the dried mushrooms by soaking in the lukewarm water for 30 minutes. Rinse them in several changes of cold water to remove any sand. Strain the soaking liquid through a sieve lined with paper towels. Set aside the mushrooms and the strained liquid.

Preheat the oven to 400°. Melt the butter in a sauté pan. When hot, add the shallots, onion, and garlic. Cook, stirring, for about 5 minutes, until the onion is golden. Add the mushrooms and their liquid and cook for 5 minutes, until the liquid evaporates. Add the tomatoes and cook for 5 to 10 minutes, until the liquid evaporates. Add salt and pepper. Let cool briefly.

The terrine is garnished with flat-leaf parsley, endive, and red bell pepper.

In a mixing bowl, combine the beef, pork, and chicken livers with the mushroom-tomato mixture. Add the remaining ingredients and blend well. Test the seasonings by sautéing a small amount of the mixture and adjust if necessary.

Transfer the mixture to a 9 × 5 × 3-inch loaf pan. Set it in a larger pan and pour enough boiling water into the larger pan to reach halfway up the sides of the loaf pan. Bake for 1 hour, until the internal temperature registers 160° on a thermometer. Let set for 15 minutes before slicing. Serve hot or at room temperature with Eggplant Caviar (recipe follows).

SERVES 6

. . . .

Eggplant Caviar

This variation of "poor man's caviar"—and not so poor with cream and eggs—is used here as a sauce. It can also be used as a dip for the pita crisps.

- 2 medium eggplants
- Salt
- Juice of ½ lemon, or to taste
- 1 medium garlic clove, finely minced
- ¼ cup heavy cream
- 3 egg yolks
- ¼ cup olive oil
- 1 tablespoon sour cream
- Paprika, to taste
- Freshly ground black pepper, to taste

Preheat the oven to 350°. Cut the eggplants in half lengthwise. Sprinkle thoroughly with salt and place, cut side up, on a baking sheet. Bake for 1 hour. Remove the eggplants, let cool slightly, and invert on to paper towels. When cool, squeeze the eggplants gently to press out any liquid.

Scrape the eggplant flesh into the work bowl of a food processor fitted with the steel blade, add the lemon juice, garlic, cream, and egg yolks, and process until well mixed. Slowly add the oil and blend in the sour cream. Season with paprika, salt, and pepper. Refrigerate until ready to serve.

SERVES 6

A crisp salad that won't wilt—perfect for a picnic.

Snow Pea, Yellow Bell Pepper, and Mushroom Salad

A pretty salad with its clear colors. Except for the mushrooms, which would turn brown, the vegetables can be prepared ahead and tossed at the picnic site.

SWEET AND SOUR DRESSING
MAKES ABOUT 1/2 CUP

- 2 teaspoons sesame oil
- 3 tablespoons white wine vinegar
- 2 tablespoons sugar
- 1/2 teaspoon salt
- 1 teaspoon freshly ground black pepper
- 1/4 cup vegetable oil

- 1/2 pound fresh snow peas, trimmed and strings removed
- 1 large yellow (or red) bell pepper, cored, seeded, ribs removed, and sliced
- 1/2 pound mushrooms, cleaned and thinly sliced
- 2 tablespoons sesame seeds, toasted (see Note, page 39)

To make the dressing, vigorously shake all the dressing ingredients together in a covered jar.

Blanch the snow peas in a large pot of salted boiling water for 1 minute. Drain and refresh under cold running water. Pat dry with paper towels. Combine the snow peas, pepper, and mushrooms in a salad bowl. Toss with enough dressing to coat and sprinkle with toasted sesame seeds.

SERVES 6

Pita Herb Triangles

Pita bread, one of the recently discovered pleasures from the Middle East, is available almost everywhere.

- 8 tablespoons (1 stick) unsalted butter, melted
- 1 tablespoon fresh rosemary or 1 teaspoon dried
- 1 tablespoon fresh oregano or 1 teaspoon dried
- 1 tablespoon fresh thyme or 1 teaspoon dried
- 4 snack-size pita breads (5 to 6 inches in diameter)

Combine the butter with the herbs and let stand for 1 hour or more, to allow the flavors to meld.

Preheat the oven to 300°. Slice open the pita breads horizontally to make 8 pieces. Brush with the herb butter. Cut each piece into 6 wedges and place on a baking sheet. Bake for 18 to 20 minutes, until crisp.

MAKES 48 PIECES

Toasted pita triangles are good by themselves or dipped into the eggplant caviar.

Lemon Tart with Grand Marnier Cream

A California interpretation of a classic lemon tart. The Grand Marnier cream makes it elegant enough for a Grand Concourse picnic.

PASTRY CRUST

1½ cups unbleached all-purpose flour
¼ cup sugar
 Pinch of salt
10 tablespoons (1¼ sticks) cold unsalted butter, cut into 5 pieces
1 egg yolk mixed with 1 tablespoon cold water

LEMON FILLING

6 egg yolks
1 cup sugar
2 teaspoons cornstarch
 Grated rind of 2 small lemons (about 2 tablespoons)
½ cup freshly squeezed and strained lemon juice

GRAND MARNIER CREAM

1 egg yolk
¼ cup sifted confectioners' sugar
2 tablespoons Grand Marnier
1 cup sour cream

GARNISH

 Thin slices of fresh lemon or lemon zest

To make the pastry, combine the flour, sugar, salt, and butter in a food processor fitted with the steel blade. Using an on-and-off motion, process until the mixture resembles coarse meal. With the motor running, add the egg yolk mixed with water through the feed tube. Process just until the dough begins to hold together; do not let it form a ball. Turn the dough out onto plastic wrap, press into a flat disk, and refrigerate for at least 1 hour. On a lightly floured board, or between two sheets of plastic wrap, roll out the chilled dough to a thickness of ¼ inch. Line a 9-inch tart pan with a removable bottom with the pastry. Pressing it firmly into the pan, roll a rolling pin over the edge to remove any excess dough. Prick the bottom with a fork. Refrigerate until firm.

Preheat the oven to 400°. Place aluminum foil over the tart shell and fill with pie weights or beans. Bake for 10 minutes. Remove the foil and weights and return the shell to the oven for 10 to 15 minutes more, until lightly browned. Let cool on a rack.

To make the filling, whip the egg yolks and sugar to form a ribbon, about 2 to 3 minutes. Add the cornstarch, lemon rind, and lemon juice and mix until smooth. Pour into the cooled tart shell and bake for 18 to 20 minutes. If the edges become too brown, tent the tart with alumium foil. Let cool to room temperature.

To make the cream, mix the egg yolk and confectioners' sugar, add the Grand Marnier and sour cream, and stir well. Spoon a generous amount of cream over the tart. Garnish with lemon slices or zest, if desired.

MAKES ONE 9-INCH TART

Pretty with its thin-sliced lemon garnish, delicious splashed with Grand Marnier cream, this is an aristocratic tart that travels well.

SAN FRANCISCO BAY

In their eagerness to find China, which they firmly believed would be just around the next luff, early mariners kept sailing past San Francisco Bay. It was not until 1775—262 years after Balboa discovered the Pacific Ocean, and 242 years after Hernando Cortés found and named California—that Don Manuel Ayala brought the first ship through the Golden Gate. It must have been quite a moment.

It is, of course, one of the magnificent bays of the world, and its people stay close to it, some by living on an island—such as Belvedere or Tiburon. Generally, these are boating people, ignoring the modern causeway and riding to the city on the local ferry.

It may have taken a while to find it, but boats now skim the Bay in flocks like white-winged pigeons in Piazza San Marco. A San Francisco lunch was carried aboard the schooner *Mistral*—a schooner being defined as a ship with two or more masts, rigged fore and aft—on a fine and windy day. A mixed seafood salad included Dungeness crab, a San Francisco glory when it is available. Sourdough bread accompanied, and a fresh fruit tart followed. No one is quite sure what makes San Francisco sourdough different from all other sourdough breads. The climate? Brick ovens? Whatever, it is wonderful, and quite essential for a true San Francisco experience.

The dressing for the salad is made with raspberry vinegar and balsamic vinegar, two fairly recent California passions. Balsamic vinegar is made in Italy from wine in a lengthy (12-year) process of aging and blending in different woods, similar to the solera method of making sherry. It has a marvelous strong, dark, and complex flavor.

LUNCH ON DECK

FOR **4**

Mussel, Crab, and Scallop Salad with Mixed Vegetables

Sourdough Bread

Mango-Plum Tart

Iced Tea with Lemon

Grey or Johannesburg Riesling

. . . .

Mussel, Crab, and Scallop Salad with Mixed Vegetables

A hearty, seafaring salad, which allows all sorts of substitutions according to market availability. With fresh shellfish and a balanced combination of the vegetables, pasta, and seafood, it is delicious—even without a sail on San Francisco Bay to whet the appetite.

½ pound bay scallops

½ pound small mussels, scrubbed and debearded (discard any open ones), or cooked bay shrimp, or a combination of both

½ pound tiny red potatoes, unpeeled

⅓ pound haricots verts or tender young string beans, trimmed and cut into 2-inch lengths

½ pound yellow or red baby beets, trimmed but unpeeled

1 cup gemelli or fusilli (available in Italian markets)

DRESSING

¼ cup raspberry vinegar

1 teaspoon balsamic vinegar

⅔ cup extra virgin olive oil

Salt and freshly ground black pepper, to taste

½ pound crab meat (preferably Alaska king or Dungeness crab)

1 cup corn kernels (from 2 ears of corn)

1 10-ounce can of artichoke hearts, rinsed and dried

½ large head of red leaf lettuce, torn into bite-size pieces

1 large head of Boston lettuce, torn into bite-size pieces

2 heads of Belgian endive, leaves separated, and cut in half lengthwise, if desired

Bounty from the sea and the garden—just right for a lunch on deck.

Cook the scallops in boiling salted water for 1 minute. Drain immediately, let cool, and set aside. Steam the mussels for about 5 minutes, just until their shells open. Let cool, remove from the shell, and set aside.

Put the potatoes in a pot of cold salted water. Bring to a boil and cook for about 15 minutes, just until tender. Rinse with cold water, and cut into halves or quarters. Blanch the haricots verts in boiling salted water for 3 minutes, refresh under cold water, and drain well. Cook the beets in boiling salted water for 5 to 10 minutes, depending on their size. Peel and drain well.

Cook the pasta in 2 quarts of boiling salted water until al dente. Rinse with cold water. Drain and toss with a little vegetable oil to keep the pasta from sticking.

To make the dressing, combine the vinegars in a bowl and slowly whisk in the olive oil. Add salt and pepper.

To assemble, gently toss the scallops, potatoes, beans, and pasta with the crab meat, corn, artichoke hearts, greens, and enough dressing to coat. Place on individual plates and arrange the beets and mussels on top. Drizzle on additional dressing. Serve immediately.

VARIATION: For a different presentation, the mussels may be left in their shells and arranged on the salad.

SERVES 4

Mango-Plum Tart

Puff pastry, a necessary skill for the California cook, is less time-consuming with this simplified recipe. This deceptively innocent luxury can also add distinction to vegetables, sauced meats, and many other things.

MOCK PUFF PASTRY (SEE NOTE)

1½   cups unbleached all-purpose flour
½   teaspoon salt
14   tablespoons (1¾ sticks) cold unsalted butter, cut into ¼-inch dice
¼   cup cold water

PASTRY CREAM

½   cup milk
½   cup heavy cream
3   egg yolks
¼   cup sugar
½   teaspoon vanilla extract
1½   tablespoons cornstarch

RHUBARB GLAZE

⅓   cup rhubarb jam (apricot jam may be substituted)
2   tablespoons water

1   mango, peeled and thinly sliced lengthwise
3 or 4 plums, thinly sliced

To make the puff pastry, put the flour and salt in a food processor fitted with the steel blade and pulse the machine on and off 3 times. Add the butter and pulse 3 to 5 times, until the mixture is very crumbly but not yet a dough. Turn the machine on, pour in the cold water, then immediately turn it off. Transfer the mixture to a sheet of wax paper and gently pat it into a rectangle. At this point the dough will still look messy. Cover tightly with plastic wrap or wax paper and refrigerate for 45 minutes, or freeze for 20 minutes.

Turn the dough out onto a lightly floured surface. Quickly roll it into a long rectangle, ⅜ inch thick. Dust off any excess flour with a brush. If the pastry sticks to the rolling pin, return it to the refrigerator until it is easy to handle.

Starting with one of the short sides of the rectangle in front of you, fold the dough into thirds by folding the bottom third over the middle third and then folding the top third down over both, as if folding a letter. You have now completed the first turn.

Rotate the dough 90° so that the short side is facing you and the long side is open on the right. Working quickly, lightly press down the dough with a rolling pin and roll it out to a ⅜-inch-thick rectangle. Again fold the dough into thirds. The second turn is now complete. Press two fingertips into the dough to remind you that two turns have been made. Wrap the dough in plastic wrap or wax paper and chill for 30 minutes.

Roll out and make two more turns of the dough, beating the dough up and down and back and forth evenly with your rolling pin if it is hard to roll. Chill for another 30 minutes and complete two more turns, for a total of six turns. Refrigerate until needed. The dough may be frozen, wrapped airtight, for up to 6 months.

To make the pastry cream, bring the milk and cream to a boil. Set aside. Whisk the egg yolks, sugar, and vanilla together until the mixture is light and thick. Mix in the cornstarch and beat in the milk-cream mixture. Transfer to a heavy saucepan and slowly bring to a boil, stirring constantly. The custard will thicken as it reaches the boiling point. Remove from the heat, strain if necessary, and let cool. If not using immediately, cover and refrigerate.

To assemble and bake the tart, preheat the oven to 400°. Heat the rhubarb jam, strain it, and combine with the water. Remove the puff pastry from the refrigerator and on a floured board roll it out to a 9 × 14-inch rectangle. Spread about ⅔ cup pastry cream down the center of the tart, leaving a border of about 1 inch. Arrange the mango and plum slices decoratively on top of the pastry cream. Brush the fruit only with rhubarb glaze. Line a baking sheet with parchment and bake the tart on it in the bottom third of the oven for 15 to 20 minutes, until the pastry is golden and puffed. Remove from the oven and brush the entire tart with additional glaze. Serve warm or at room temperature.

NOTE: Frozen all-butter puff pastry may be used according to package directions.

MAKES ONE 9 × 14-INCH TART

A magnificent swirl of fresh fruit colors and flavors in a long shell of puff pastry.

D E S E R T

California's deserts are extraordinarily beautiful and among the most famous in the world. In summer, the sun shines with particular brilliance. In winter, the air is so clear it cannot be seen, only felt in its brittle serenity; miles become inches in the transparency. The changing colors of the desert, held all around in the shadowed blues of the high, bare mountains, are as endlessly fascinating as the shifting tides of the sea.

Long ago, these vast, seemingly endless stretches of land were inhabited by little more than wildlife and exotic vegetation. Today, the desert is a place for luxurious living in California. There are magnificent homes, exclusive shops, fashionable resorts and spas, golf courses, tennis courts, a marvelous sense of leisure, and, of course, an informed interest in food. Dates are the major contribution to gastronomy; ninety percent of the country's supply comes from the Coachella Valley. Fresh-picked and eaten there, they are wonderful.

The desert provides one more facet to California's extraordinary lifestyle, the drama and tempo reflected in the subtle differences of its way with California cooking.

Palm Desert

. . . .

Sometimes it seems as though California were meant for play, there are so many ways to enjoy yourself. One could almost drive a golf ball from one course to the next, never stopping from one end of the state to the other. (There are sixty golf courses near Palm Springs.) Tennis courts are everywhere, and swimmers can dive into anything from the ocean to natural hot springs, with a few million pools around as alternatives. There are fields for polo, trails for riding, mountains for climbing and skiing, bays, lakes, and an ocean for sailing and water-skiing and fishing. It is possible to jog, ice-skate, roller-skate, or bicycle; to play baseball, handball, volleyball, jai alai; or to practice jujitsu, yoga, karate, or aerobic dancing.

Hot-air ballooning in the desert is the most recent addition to this roster of activity. It does not supplant golf, tennis, or any of the other exertions, but rather augments them. Floating through the air is not only sporting but restful—a shower for the senses, one might say. The desert is a splendid place for the bright-colored bubbles, offering lovely crosscurrents for adventurous floating—and the scenery is marvelous. (Hot-air balloons are also a passion in the Napa Valley, where breezes are equally obliging.)

Even cooking has become a way to play in California, a duty become a pleasure, appealing as much to men as to women. Skill in the kitchen is as honorable as skill on the tennis court.

A tailgate picnic, to be ready when the balloon came down and the passengers floated out, exhilarated and hungry, was the challenge presented our hosts. They solved it nicely with dishes that traveled well and were more appealing cold than hot. The same menu could, of course, go with equal success to other playful places.

TAILGATE PICNIC

FOR **6**

Minted Grapefruit Cooler

Fruited Chicken Salad with Tarragon Mayonnaise

Cold Beef Salad with Caper Vinaigrette

Dill Bread

Breakaway Cookie

Pinot Noir Blanc

. . . .

Minted Grapefruit Cooler

A thirst quencher—particularly refreshing when served icy-cold.

3½ **cups freshly squeezed and strained grapefruit juice**

2 **tablespoons sugar, or to taste**

6 **sprigs mint, and additional mint for garnishing**

6 **tablespoons freshly squeezed and strained lemon juice**

3½ **cups ginger ale**

Combine the grapefruit juice, sugar, and mint in a pitcher. Let sit for several hours or overnight. Just before serving, add the lemon juice and ginger ale. Fill glasses with ice cubes and pour in the grapefruit–ginger ale mixture. Garnish with fresh mint. Serve immediately.

SERVES 6

One balloon is down and others are floating in, brilliant against the sky. Passengers are exhilarated by their drift over the desert—and hungry. In the station wagon, food is ready in baskets and wooden bowls.

Chicken salad garnished with fresh pear.

Fruited Chicken Salad with Tarragon Mayonnaise

A salad that can be varied in many ways, according to the market. Melon, avocado, kiwi, or oranges would be interesting additions or substitutions. If it is to be tailgated for any length of time, it should be carried on ice.

TARRAGON MAYONNAISE
MAKES ABOUT 2 CUPS

- 2 extra-large eggs, at room temperature
- 2 teaspoons freshly squeezed lemon juice
- 2 teaspoons tarragon vinegar
- 1 teaspoon dry mustard
- 1 teaspoon dried tarragon
- ¾ teaspoon curry powder
- 1½ to 2 teaspoons salt
  - Freshly ground white pepper, to taste
- 2 cups vegetable oil

FRUITED CHICKEN SALAD

- 4 whole chicken breasts
- 2 quarts chicken stock, preferably homemade (page 17), or water
- 2 celery stalks, cut into fine julienne
- ¾ cup seedless green grapes
- ½ cup golden raisins
- ½ cup dried pitted prunes, cut crosswise into ⅛-inch slices
- 1 bunch of chives, snipped
- ½ cup coarsely chopped macadamia nuts
  - Salt and freshly ground black pepper, to taste

  - Boston lettuce cups

GARNISH
- Slices of lime, melon, peaches, or pears

To make the mayonnaise, combine the eggs, lemon juice, vinegar, mustard, and seasonings in a food processor fitted with the steel blade. With the machine running, drizzle in the vegetable oil drop by drop. As the mayonnaise begins to thicken, oil may be added a little faster. Adjust the seasonings. Refrigerate until needed.

To make the salad, poach the chicken breasts, partially covered in simmering chicken broth or water, for 15 to 20 minutes, until tender. Do not overcook. Remove from the stock and let cool. Remove the skin and bones, and cut the chicken into 1-inch cubes. Add the other salad ingredients and gently toss with enough tarragon mayonnaise to coat well. Add salt and pepper, if necessary. Serve the salad in lettuce cups garnished with fruit slices, if desired.

SERVES 6 TO 8

. . . .

Cold Beef Salad with Caper Vinaigrette

A fine hearty salad that travels well. Carry the vinaigrette in a jar and toss with the assembled ingredients just before serving.

- 1½ pounds boneless sirloin steak, 1 inch thick

CAPER VINAIGRETTE
MAKES ABOUT 2 CUPS

- 4 teaspoons capers
- 3 tablespoons lemon juice
- ½ cup red wine vinegar
- 4 teaspoons Dijon-style mustard
- 1 cup vegetable oil
- ½ cup extra virgin olive oil
- ¾ teaspoon salt
- ¼ teaspoon freshly ground black pepper

- ¾ pound haricots verts or very young string beans, trimmed
- ½ pound fresh mushrooms, cleaned and thinly sliced
- 3 medium tomatoes, peeled and cut into wedges
- ½ red onion, cut in thin slivers
- ¾ cup thinly sliced canned hearts of palm, cut into 2-inch lengths
- 1 bunch of watercress, bottom stems removed

GARNISH
- 3 tablespoons chopped fresh oregano
- 3 tablespoons chopped fresh thyme

Broil or barbecue the steak for 5 minutes on each side, until medium rare. Let cool slightly. Cut into thin slices, about ½ inch × 2½ inches.

Combine the vinaigrette ingredients in a glass jar and shake well to combine. Use about a third of it to marinate the meat slices for an hour or more before serving.

In a pot of boiling water, blanch the haricots verts for 3 to 4 minutes, until crisp-tender. Refresh under cold water and drain well. Set aside. Blanch the red onion for 20 seconds in boiling water. Refresh under cold water and set aside.

To serve, remove the meat from the marinade and combine with the other salad ingredients in a bowl. Toss with enough vinaigrette to coat. Garnish with chopped oregano and thyme, and serve at room temperature.

SERVES 6

A hearty cold beef salad served with homemade dill bread.

Dill Bread

Fine for a picnic, as it can be made quickly, does not need time to rise, and can be served at any temperature.

 3 **cups self-rising flour**
 3 **tablespoons light brown sugar**
 1 **tablespoon dried dillweed**
 1 **12-ounce can of light beer**
 4 **tablespoons (½ stick) unsalted butter, melted**

Preheat the oven to 375°. Grease a 9 × 5-inch loaf pan. In an electric mixer, combine the flour, brown sugar, and dillweed. Mix well. Add the beer and blend again. Pour into the loaf pan and pour the melted butter over the top. Bake for 50 to 55 minutes. Turn out the loaf and tap it on the bottom. When done, it will sound hollow. Do not overbake. Transfer to a cooling rack. Serve warm, at room temperature, or toasted.

MAKES 1 LOAF

An oversize cookie for everyone to share.

Breakaway Cookie

A very good, quite simple, giant almond cookie, which could also be made in people sizes.

 ½ **cup finely ground almonds**
 1⅓ **cups unbleached all-purpose flour**
 ½ **cup sugar**
 Pinch of salt
 1 **tablespoon freshly squeezed lemon juice**
 1½ **tablespoons grated lemon rind**
 9 **tablespoons unsalted butter, at room temperature**
 1½ **tablespoons amaretto liqueur**

Preheat the oven to 325°. Butter and flour an 11- or 12-inch tart pan with a removable bottom.

In a large bowl, mix the almonds, flour, sugar, salt, lemon juice, lemon rind, and butter with a fork. Sprinkle with the liqueur and mix lightly. The dough should be crumbly.

Using your fingertips, spread the mixture evenly in the pan. Do not press down. Bake for 30 to 40 minutes, until lightly browned. Let cool in the pan on a rack. When cool, cover with aluminum foil and let sit at room temperature for a day to mellow.

To serve, transfer to a serving plate and let guests break off pieces to nibble.

MAKES ONE 11- TO 12-INCH COOKIE

RANCHO MIRAGE

. . . .

There is a special technique to desert living. Set against gray-blue mountains and tawny sands, constantly changing with light and shadow, colors need to be strong but cool and steady, lines straight. Nature favors the spare lines and sharp angles of the cactus and the palm tree.

This Rancho Mirage home has a suggestion of the Moorish in the squared columns and roof lines, while the granite lounging chairs are reminiscent of Egypt. It is visually cooled by the deep blue of the tiles in the pool. The patio is shaded against the sun, but open to any stray breeze.

One eats lightly in the desert. It is not the place for hearty stews and rich desserts; salads and fruits are best in the midday heat, and not much more for the warm evening. But the food need not—and should not—therefore be dull; finicky appetites need to be titillated. This requires only a little imagination to ensure variety. A new taste in an herb or green can completely change a dish. An unusual juxtaposition of familiar flavors means a new experience.

The chicken and turnip luncheon salad meets these requirements nicely. Both the turnips and the hazelnut oil in the dressing are unusual, and radicchio is a cool, strong accent. Until recently, turnips have been more favored in Europe than in this country, and no wonder. They used to arrive on our tables in a pale, watery mash with a strong flavor children learned to hate. But contemporary cooking uses young, sweet turnips. Boiled briefly to preserve their crispness, they can be as refreshing as an apple.

The grilled duck livers with pearl onions and apples on a bed of greens is a hearty salad admirably suited to a desert supper.

The brilliance of saffron consommé (left), and the cool heartiness of duck liver salad (right), are set off by the high colors of Fiestaware.

EARLY SUPPER

FOR 6

Saffron Consommé

Ribbon Rolls

Grilled Duck Liver Salad with
Pearl Onions and Apples

Lemon Ice Cream   •   **S**and Dollars

White Zinfandel

. . . .

Saffron Consommé

With a white stock ready and waiting in the freezer, this bright, clear soup is simple to put together. Saffron adds its bright color and a taste of luxury.

> 9 **cups White Stock (page 92)**
> 3 **egg whites**
> 3 **eggshells, crushed**
> 3 **tablespoons grated onion**
> ¾ **teaspoon saffron threads or ½ scant teaspoon ground saffron**
> **Salt and freshly ground white pepper, to taste**

In a large saucepan, bring the stock to a boil over high heat. Meanwhile, in a small bowl, whisk the egg whites until frothy. Stir the egg whites and shells into the boiling stock, reduce the heat, and simmer gently, without stirring, for 20 minutes. Strain the stock into another saucepan through a large sieve lined with several thicknesses of rinsed cheesecloth, and bring to a simmer over moderate heat. Put the grated onion in a fine sieve over a small bowl and press with the back of a spoon to extract the juice. Measure 2 teaspoons of onion juice and add to the stock.

If using saffron threads, crush them between your fingers and put in a small dish. Add a little stock, stir gently to dissolve, and add to the simmering stock. If using ground saffron, whisk it directly into the stock.

Simmer for 5 minutes more, to let the flavors blend. Add salt and pepper. Serve hot.

SERVES 6 TO 8

White Stock

Making a stock is a rewarding occupation on a cold winter day. Four stocks are included in this book, and with the four ready in the freezer, there are no limits to the possibilities.

- 2 pounds chicken parts (backs, wings, necks)
- 2 pounds veal shanks, cut into 2-inch pieces
- 3 quarts water
- 1 large carrot, peeled, trimmed, and cut into 1-inch pieces
- 1 celery stalk with leaves, trimmed and cut into 1-inch pieces
- 2 medium leeks, trimmed, cleaned, and cut into 1-inch pieces
- 1 medium onion, peeled and halved
- 2 cloves
- 6 sprigs of parsley
- ½ teaspoon dried thyme
- 1 bay leaf
- ½ teaspoon freshly ground white pepper

Put the chicken and veal in a stockpot and add enough water to cover by about 2 inches. Bring to a boil, reduce the heat, and simmer, uncovered, for 5 minutes. Drain and rinse the meat under cold running water to remove all of the scum. Rinse the pot and wipe it clean.

Return the meat to the stockpot and add the 3 quarts water. Bring to a boil over high heat, skimming often. Add the remaining ingredients. Reduce the heat, partially cover, and simmer very gently for 3 hours. Skim occasionally.

Strain the stock into a large container through a double layer of rinsed cheesecloth. Let cool, then refrigerate. Remove the fat from the surface when it coagulates. The stock may be refrigerated, covered, for 3 or 4 days. It may be frozen for up to 6 months.

MAKES APPROXIMATELY 2½ QUARTS

Ribbon rolls are appetizing and unusual.

Ribbon Rolls

Tomato juice adds color as well as a slightly different flavor to these pretty rolls.

WHITE DOUGH
- ½ package active dry yeast
- 2 tablespoons sugar
- ½ cup plus 2 tablespoons lukewarm water (105° to 115°)
- 1 egg, beaten
- 4 tablespoons (½ stick) unsalted butter, melted
- 2¼ to 2½ cups unbleached all-purpose flour
- 1 teaspoon salt

RED DOUGH
- ½ package active dry yeast
- 2 tablespoons sugar
- 2 tablespoons lukewarm water (105° to 115°)
- ½ cup tomato juice, heated to lukewarm (105° to 115°)
- 1 egg, beaten
- 4 tablespoons (½ stick) unsalted butter, melted
- 2¼ to 2½ cups unbleached all-purpose flour
- 1 teaspoon salt

GLAZE
- 1 egg, beaten
- 1 tablespoon celery seeds (optional)

To make the white dough, dissolve the yeast and ½ teaspoon sugar in the 2 tablespoons lukewarm water. Set aside until the mixture becomes foamy.

In a large mixing bowl, combine the remaining ½ cup lukewarm water, the egg, the remaining sugar, and the melted butter. Blend in the yeast mixture. Mix the flour and salt together and add 1 cup at a time, until you have a soft dough. Knead on a floured board for 5 to 8 minutes, until smooth and elastic. Place in an oiled bowl and turn to coat the dough. Cover with a towel and let rise in a warm, draft-free place for 1 hour, until doubled.

For the red dough, follow the same directions as for the white, substituting tomato juice for the ½ cup water.

When both doughs have doubled in size, punch them down. Divide each into 12 pieces, and roll each piece into a 6- to 8-inch-long rope. Twist one white dough rope and one red dough rope together. Cut into 2-inch lengths and pinch the ends together. Repeat with the remaining dough. Place the twists on a greased baking sheet, cover with a towel, and let rise in a warm, draft-free place for 1 hour, until doubled.

Preheat the oven to 350°. Brush each twist with the beaten egg. Sprinkle with celery seeds, if desired. Bake for 12 to 15 minutes, until golden brown. Let cool on a rack. The rolls may be frozen, wrapped airtight.

VARIATION: If you wish to make small breads instead of rolls, make the ropes thicker, about 1 inch in diameter, and prepare in the same manner as for rolls.

MAKES 36 TO 48 ROLLS

. . . .

Grilled Duck Liver Salad with Pearl Onions and Apples

Have the butcher save duck livers for you. The greens are light, the liver hearty, and the apples refreshing.

24	pearl onions, peeled (see Note, page 200)
3	tablespoons olive oil
6	tablespoons (¾ stick) unsalted butter
6	tablespoons sugar
½	pound slab bacon, rind removed and cut across the grain into 1-inch × ½-inch pieces
1¼	pounds duck livers
	Salt and freshly ground black pepper, to taste
2	large garlic cloves, unpeeled
2	large tart apples (such as Granny Smith), unpeeled, cored, and cut into ¼-inch-thick slices
1	large head of escarole, cut into chiffonade
1	large head of Boston lettuce, torn into bite-size pieces
4	cups mache (lamb's lettuce), torn into bite-size pieces
¾	cup extra virgin olive oil
3	tablespoons sherry vinegar

GARNISH

2	teaspoons chopped fresh thyme or snipped chives

Heat 3 tablespoons olive oil in a large skillet. When hot, add the onions and sauté until nicely browned. Add the butter and sugar, reduce the heat to low, and toss the onions until they are well coated. Cook, stirring occasionally, for 10 to 15 minutes, until glazed. Set aside and keep warm.

Cover the bacon with water, bring to a boil, reduce the heat, and poach for 2 minutes to firm it up and extract excess fat. Drain and sauté the bacon until crisp. Set aside.

Heat a grill or sauté pan and brush lightly with oil. Season the duck livers with salt and pepper and cook until medium rare. Slice ¼ inch thick on the diagonal and keep warm. Sauté the garlic in a little olive oil until softened and browned. Peel, mince, and set aside. If necessary, re-oil the grill or sauté pan lightly, and grill the apple slices until lightly browned. Set aside and keep warm.

Toss the escarole, Boston lettuce, and mache with the ¾ cup olive oil, sherry vinegar, reserved garlic, and salt and pepper. To serve, place the greens on a plate and arrange the liver, onions, and apples on top. Sprinkle with the bacon, and thyme or chives if desired. Serve warm or at room temperature.

SERVES 6 AS A MAIN COURSE

Ice cream and cookies—a classic combination.

Sand Dollars

An excellent, buttery cookie that is good to have on hand all the time. Especially good with ice cream.

1	cup (2 sticks) unsalted butter, at room temperature
1	cup sugar
1½	cups unbleached all-purpose flour
½	teaspoon baking soda
1	scant teaspoon salt
½	teaspoon distilled vinegar

Preheat the oven to 350°. Cream the butter and sugar together, and blend in the rest of the ingredients. Drop rounded teaspoons of dough, 2 inches apart, on an ungreased baking sheet and press into 2½- to 3-inch rounds using a flat-bottomed glass dipped in water, then sugar. Bake for 12 to 15 minutes, until golden brown around the edges. Remove from the baking sheet immediately and let cool on a rack.

MAKES 36 COOKIES

LUNCH BY THE POOL

FOR **4**

Warm Chicken and Turnips in
Hazelnut Oil Vinaigrette

Salt, Sesame, or Poppy Seed Breadsticks

Papaya and Blueberries with Lime Sabayon

Blanc de Noir Sparkling

. . . .

Cactus thrusts from a stone bowl on the cool granite table. In keeping with the setting, the chicken salad arrives on a thick, unpolished marble tray.

Warm Chicken and Turnips in Hazelnut Oil Vinaigrette

Radicchio is a red winter lettuce, a specialty of Treviso, Italy. It has a sweet, peppery flavor—like eating flowers, they say in Treviso—and brightens almost any salad. Most specialty markets and some supermarkets now have it.

2 whole chicken breasts, skinned, split, and boned

1 tablespoon unsalted butter

8 turnips (2 to 3 inches in diameter), peeled and thinly sliced (4 to 5 cups)

3 tablespoons hazelnut oil (walnut oil may be substituted)

Salt and freshly ground white pepper, to taste

HAZELNUT OIL VINAIGRETTE
MAKES ABOUT 1 CUP

2½ tablespoons red wine vinegar

½ to 1 teaspoon salt

Freshly ground white pepper

1 cup hazelnut oil (walnut oil may be substituted)

1 or 2 small heads of radicchio, washed and dried

1 large shallot, finely minced

1 bunch of chives, snipped

Melt the butter in a skillet. Cook the chicken, uncovered, over *very* low heat until tender (about 40 minutes), adding more butter if necessary. Let cool in the juices. When cool, slice the breasts thinly on the diagonal. Reserve the juices.

While the chicken is cooling, sauté the turnips in the hazelnut oil until barely tender. Add salt and pepper, and set aside.

To make the vinaigrette, whisk together the vinegar, salt, and pepper in a small bowl. Add the oil slowly, stirring constantly, until smooth and well blended.

Mix the turnips with ¾ cup of the vinaigrette and reserve the remainder.

To assemble the salad, decorate a platter or individual plates with the radicchio and arrange the turnips on top. Place the chicken slices on the turnips and sprinkle with the shallot and chives. Pour the reserved chicken juices and the remaining vinaigrette over the chicken, and serve warm or at room temperature.

SERVES 4

Salt, Sesame, or Poppy
Seed Breadsticks

Lean and crisp, these breadsticks are particularly suitable for a hot day. They can be baked ahead and frozen.

1 recipe Pizza Dough (page 106)
1 egg, beaten with 1 tablespoon water
  Coarse salt
  Sesame seeds
  Poppy seeds

Make the pizza dough according to the instructions and let it rest, covered with a towel, for 20 to 30 minutes.

Shape the dough into a roll 20 to 22 inches long. Cut the roll into 1-inch-long pieces. Let it rest for 3 to 4 minutes and then, with the palms of your hands, roll each piece as evenly as possible into a stick the length of your baking sheet. Cut the sticks in half if you want to make short breadsticks.

Preheat the oven to 350°. Lightly oil 2 or 3 baking sheets. Place the sticks 1 inch apart on the sheets. Brush with the egg and sprinkle with either salt, sesame seeds, or poppy seeds.

Bake for 30 to 40 minutes, until browned and crisp. Let cool on a rack. Store wrapped airtight.

MAKES 20 LONG OR 40 SHORT STICKS

Desert life can be sybaritic, when there's a couch to recline on and a glass of sparkling wine within reach. The plates are handmade and handpainted by a Los Angeles artist.

Papaya and Blueberries
with Lime Sabayon

The sabayon is simple to prepare, with lime and cream as refreshing variations to the usual white wine.

1 large papaya, peeled and seeded
1 pint fresh blueberries or one 10-ounce package of frozen blueberries, defrosted

LIME SABAYON
2 egg yolks
¼ cup sugar
  Grated rind and juice of 2 limes
½ cup heavy cream, lightly whipped

GARNISH
  Lime slices

Cut the papaya lengthwise into 12 slices and arrange the slices on 4 serving plates. Scatter blueberries on top of the papaya and set aside while you prepare the lime sabayon.

Whisk the egg yolks and sugar together in the top of a double boiler until thick and pale yellow. Stir in the lime juice and combine well. Place over barely simmering water and cook for 8 minutes, stirring constantly with a whisk, until the mixture thickens and becomes creamy. Remove the top of the double boiler from the heat and immediately place it in a bowl of ice water. Whisk the sabayon until it cools to room temperature. Fold in the grated lime rind and whipped cream, and spoon the sauce over the fruit. Garnish each plate with lime slices.

SERVES 4

**Papaya and blueberries make this
sabayon a very pretty dessert.**

C I T Y

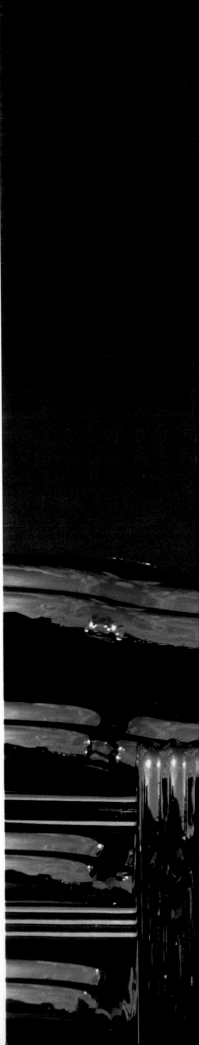

Regional cuisines historically have developed from the bounty of the land and the tastes of the people, brightened by ingenuity and whatever fresh ideas were introduced from elsewhere. This instinctive cooking ultimately was refined and elaborated by professional chefs to become haute cuisine.

California cooking, on the other hand, is a true child of the cities, born sophisticated and almost purely intellectual. It was instantly acclaimed. New restaurants sprang up everywhere, cooking classes proliferated, specialty markets and cookstores appeared where none had been before, newspapers and magazines redid their formats to make room for the latest bulletins.

It was a civilized revolution dedicated to freshness, simplicity, and freedom in the kitchen. Nowhere were these changes more apparent than in California's three major cities, though quite different in each. A spontaneous combustion of many talents, strongly influenced by the French, made for more diversity and individuality in Los Angeles than in San Francisco or San Diego, but in cities throughout California the only limitations were, and continue to be, those of sensibility, skill, and the proven principles of good cooking.

BEVERLY HILLS

In a penthouse one can be purely alone with the sky and the distance, as solitary as a ship, entirely removed from the scramble and scurry below. It does not need to be a high penthouse in Los Angeles. Only a few stories up are enough to be free of the world in this rooftop home, with its sweeping view of Century City.

The artist-owner worked with architect Frank Gehry on the design. They planned it to alert, to stimulate, and perhaps to startle. There is nothing complacent in its exuberance of many colors, its tiles designed by the artist in checkerboard squares and Aztec zigzags, the Art Deco furniture, and the confidence of creating its own style out of a kaleidoscope of many styles.

The dinner was planned for wandering, with many small things, different dishes in different rooms, so arranged that the food became a still life amid the art. Guests could nibble as they explored.

This manner of eating—called "grazing"—has become increasingly popular in this city that loves to be casual. At least a dozen restaurants offer only many small tastes, resulting in a complete meal without a structured beginning, middle, and end. Not to be confused with fast food, each bite must have its own special value. The emphasis is on quality and variety.

The Italian theme—which is also a California theme—is not a surprising choice for this menu. Essentially, it is hearty antipasto. As most of the dishes are served at room temperature, almost everything can be prepared ahead. Only the pizza requires last-minute attention.

The grazing dinner does not have to wander. It works very nicely for a small group at table, as well as avoiding the congestion of a buffet for a large party.

GRAZING DINNER

FOR **12**

Veal Carpaccio • **A**sparagus with Bagna Cauda

Fillet of Sole with Pine Nuts, Onions, and Raisins

Artichoke, Eggplant, and Goat Cheese Pizza

Fettuccine with Spinach and Tomatoes

Almond Florentines • **S**trawberries • **E**spresso

WINES:

Chardonnay with Sole and Veal

Barbera or Zinfandel with Pizza and Pasta

. . . .

Veal Carpaccio

More delicate than the usual beef carpaccio, the veal requires a more subtle dressing. There is nothing better than good olive oil scattered with splinters of fresh Parmesan.

- **1½ pounds top round of veal**
- **1 egg yolk**
  Salt and freshly ground black pepper, to taste
- **2 to 3 tablespoons freshly squeezed lemon juice**
- **1 cup extra virgin olive oil**
- **1 2-ounce piece of fresh, moist Parmesan cheese**
- **½ cup finely julienned hearts of celery,
  crisped in ice water, drained, and dried**

GARNISH
  Slivers of red pepper

  Very thin slices of French bread, toasted

Put the veal in the freezer until firm enough to slice paper-thin, or have your butcher slice it for you.

Mix the egg yolk with salt and pepper and lemon juice. Whisk in the oil, a little at a time, until emulsified. (Do not use a food processor or the dressing will be too thick.)

Ladle three quarters of the dressing onto a large serving dish or platter. Layer the veal on top in overlapping slices. If desired, season with additional salt and pepper. Spoon on the remaining dressing. Make cheese curls by peeling paper-thin slices from the piece of Parmesan. Scatter these and the julienned celery over the top of the dish. Garnish with slivered red pepper, if desired. Let sit for at least 30 minutes at room temperature. Serve with toasted French bread.

SERVES 12

Sparkling wine is ready by the swirling hot tub with a panoramic view of Century City (above). Veal carpaccio and thinly sliced French bread are served on an inlaid tile table brightened by flowers (right).

Asparagus with Bagna Cauda

Asparagus is the most decorative of vegetables. The bagna cauda is an enriched translation of the traditional Piedmont dish, using cream instead of olive oil. It is also good as a sauce over hot vegetables.

3	to 4 pounds medium asparagus spears, well trimmed, and peeled, if desired
2	cups heavy cream
4	tablespoons (½ stick) unsalted butter
1½	teaspoons anchovy paste
1	teaspoon minced garlic

GARNISH
   Paper-thin slices of prosciutto

Blanch the asparagus in a large pot of boiling salted water for about 5 minutes, until just tender. Do not overcook. Refresh under cold water, drain well, and set aside until serving time.

In a heavy medium saucepan bring the cream to a boil. Cook over medium high heat, stirring occasionally, for 5 minutes, until the cream is thickened and reduced to about 1 cup.

Meanwhile, melt the butter (do not let it brown) in a small pot, preferably earthenware, and add the anchovy paste and garlic. Whisk to blend. Add the reduced cream and bring to a simmer, whisking constantly. Do not let it boil. Serve the bagna cauda warm, garnished with prosciutto, if desired. Dip the asparagus into the sauce.

SERVES 12

Asparagus spills from a glass cornucopia set on a freeform Memphis table. A bright blue pot holds bagna cauda for dipping. A painting by the owner dominates the background.

The fillet of sole is displayed on a green Fiestaware platter. The marching bird pitchers are favorites from the owner's collection.

Fillet of Sole with Pine Nuts, Onions, and Raisins

The pine nuts, onions, and raisins add a bit of flamboyance to the delicate sole, and the vinegar, wine, and honey give it the zip needed by fish at room temperature.

2½ to 3 pounds fillet of sole, cut on the
     diagonal into 1-inch-wide strips
     Unbleached all-purpose flour
½   to ¾ cup extra virgin olive oil
     Freshly ground black pepper, to taste
2   medium yellow onions, cut into slivers
6   tablespoons golden raisins, soaked in hot
     water to cover for 10 minutes and drained
¾   cup pine nuts, toasted
1½ cups dry white wine
6   tablespoons white wine vinegar
5   to 6 tablespoons honey

Dredge the sole in flour. Heat 4 to 5 tablespoons oil in a large heavy skillet over medium high heat. Sauté the fillets quickly, in batches, until golden brown, adding more oil as needed. Transfer to a large, shallow serving dish and sprinkle with pepper.

Heat an additional 3 tablespoons oil in the same skillet and sauté the onions for 8 to 10 minutes, until golden but not browned. Scatter over the fish, along with the raisins and pine nuts.

Combine the wine, vinegar, and honey and pour over the sole. Let cool to room temperature. Cover and refrigerate for 3 to 4 hours or overnight. Bring back to room temperature before serving.

SERVES 12

. . . .

Artichoke, Eggplant, and Goat Cheese Pizza

A good low-keyed version of the ever popular pizza, the goat cheese adding emphasis to the subtlety of the artichoke and the eggplant.

PIZZA DOUGH
1   package active dry yeast
2   teaspoons honey
1¼ cups lukewarm water (105° to 115°)
3¾ cups unbleached all-purpose flour
2   teaspoons salt
1   tablespoon olive oil

TOPPING
16   baby artichokes, about 2 inches long (see Note)
     Salt and freshly ground black pepper, to taste
     Approximately 1 cup extra virgin olive oil
4   Japanese eggplants, unpeeled
2   small garlic cloves, finely chopped
20   medium mushrooms, cleaned
12   to 16 ounces goat cheese
10   sprigs of fresh thyme, leaves only

Varicolored Fiestaware holds the pizza, served on the top of a small Art Deco piano that came from a '30s luxury liner. Flowers are arranged in a tall mercury glass container and Carmen Miranda pitchers.

To make the dough, combine the yeast with the honey and ¼ cup lukewarm water. Let sit until foamy, about 10 minutes. In a mixing bowl, place the flour, salt, 1 cup lukewarm water, the olive oil, and the yeast mixture. Mix well until a soft dough is formed. Transfer to a lightly floured board and knead for 6 to 8 minutes, until smooth and elastic. Cover the dough with a towel and let rest for 20 to 30 minutes. Divide the dough in half, cover with a towel, and refrigerate for up to 6 hours. The dough may also be frozen.

To make the topping, cut off the stems of the artichokes, then slice off the tops so that 1 inch of artichoke remains. Trim the base of each with a sharp paring knife. The choke does not have to be removed. Slice in half vertically and immediately place the hearts in olive oil to cover. Let marinate for 1 hour, then remove the artichoke hearts from the oil, strain, and use about 1 tablespoon of the oil (reserve the remainder) to sauté the hearts until golden, about 6 to 8 minutes. Add salt and pepper and set aside.

Slice the eggplants very thin on the diagonal. Heat 6 tablespoons of the reserved oil in a large sauté pan, and sauté the garlic and eggplant slices until the eggplant is limp. Add salt and pepper and set aside.

Thinly slice the mushrooms. Wipe out the sauté pan and add 1 to 2 tablespoons of the reserved oil. Quickly sauté the mushrooms over high heat just until golden. Add salt and pepper and set aside.

Preheat the oven to 450°. To assemble the pizzas, flatten each ball of dough into a circle. Place on a 14-inch pizza pan, preferably black. (A preheated pizza stone may also be used.) With your fingertips, stretch the dough evenly from the center to the edges, working clockwise. Keep the edges thicker than the center. Brush each pizza with olive oil and spread evenly with the sautéed artichokes, eggplant, and mushrooms. Crumble the goat cheese over the top and sprinkle with the thyme. Bake for 15 minutes, reduce the heat to 400°, and bake for 5 minutes more, until the crust is browned and the cheese is bubbly. Cut into wedges and serve immediately.

NOTE: If baby artichokes are unavailable, use the bottoms of larger artichokes cut into small pieces.

MAKES TWO 14-INCH PIZZAS

Fettuccine with Spinach and Tomatoes

The essence of this dish is freshness: fresh tomatoes, fresh basil, fresh spinach, with black olives for accent. It's even better if you make your own fettuccine.

½	cup extra virgin olive oil
1	medium garlic clove, minced
	Pinch of red pepper flakes
1	teaspoon salt
	Freshly ground black pepper, to taste
1	pound fettuccine
4	teaspoons balsamic vinegar
1	medium red onion, diced
1	3¼-ounce jar of capers, drained
1	cup dry-cured black olives, pitted and thinly sliced
1	bunch of basil, leaves only, washed, dried, and cut into strips crosswise (reserve 2 tablespoons for the garnish)
1	large bunch of spinach, stems removed, washed, dried, and coarsely chopped or torn (reserve several whole leaves)
3	pounds ripe tomatoes, seeded and diced

Combine the olive oil, garlic, red pepper flakes, salt, and pepper in a small bowl and set aside.

In a large pot of rapidly boiling salted water, cook the fettuccine until al dente. Drain and transfer to a large bowl. Toss with the olive oil mixture, add the vinegar, and toss again. Add the onion, capers, olives, and basil.

Just before serving, add the spinach and transfer the pasta to a serving bowl, which, if desired, can be lined with additional fresh spinach leaves. Top with the tomatoes, garnish with the reserved basil, and serve at room temperature.

SERVES 12

Fettuccine is served in the light-filled dining area (left) from a bowl made by a local artist. Shelves hold a collection of old California pitchers found at flea markets and antiques shows. Florentines (right) are oversized so that guests can break off as much as they want. Ripe strawberries are served on the side.

Almond Florentines

These lovely, wicked cookies are simple to make, impossible to resist. Serve with huge ripe strawberries, stems on, and tiny cups of espresso.

1	cup (2 sticks) unsalted butter
1	cup sugar
6	tablespoons mild honey
6	tablespoons heavy cream
1	pound slivered blanched almonds
12	ounces semisweet or bittersweet chocolate

Preheat the oven to 375°. Spray six 8-inch round aluminum-foil cake pans or thirty 3-inch tartlet pans with vegetable cooking spray.

In a heavy saucepan, combine the butter, sugar, honey, and cream. Cook over medium heat, stirring frequently, and bring to a boil. Cook at a boil for exactly 1½ minutes, stirring constantly. Remove from the heat and stir in the almonds. Divide the mixture evenly among the cake or tartlet pans, using your fingers dipped in cold water to flatten.

Bake for 10 to 12 minutes (individual tartlet pans can be placed on baking sheets). When done, the cookies should be golden brown around the edges and lighter in the center (smaller cookies will be more evenly colored). Let cool in the pans (the cookies will harden as they cool). Place the pans in the freezer for 5 to 10 minutes, then remove. Release the cookies by pressing gently on the back of the pans. Tap out, if necessary.

Melt the chocolate over hot water and let cool slightly. With a spoon, spread chocolate on the back of each cookie. Store in the refrigerator or freezer.

MAKES SIX 8-INCH OR THIRTY 3-INCH COOKIES

BREAKFAST IN BED

FOR **2**

Pink Grapefruit Sections

Shirred Eggs with Oyster, Leek, and Saffron Sauce

Assorted Toast or Rolls

Peppered Beef Bacon

Sparkling White Zinfandel

Freshly Brewed Coffee

· · · · · · · · · · · · · · · ·

Shirred Eggs with Oyster, Leek, and Saffron Sauce

An aristocratic and very distant relative of the legendary Hangtown Fry, which, with its eggs and oysters, was the most expensive dish in the California mining towns of '49.

    2 teaspoons unsalted butter
    1 small leek (white part only), thinly sliced
    6 shucked oysters, drained, with their liquor
       reserved (or a combination of the liquor and clam
       juice to equal 2 tablespoons)
    ¾ cup heavy cream
       Pinch of saffron threads, dissolved in a
       few drops of boiling water
       Salt and freshly ground white pepper, to taste
    4 eggs
       Unsalted butter, melted

Preheat the oven to 350°. In a small frying pan, heat the 2 teaspoons butter and cook the leek over medium heat for 3 minutes, until softened but not browned. Add the drained oysters, increase the heat to medium high, and cook for 2 to 3 minutes, just until the oysters are curled and heated through. Keep warm.

Over medium heat, reduce the cream by half, add the oyster liquor, and scald. Add the oyster-leek mixture, saffron, and salt and pepper. Keep warm.

Grease 2 individual ramekins or other small baking dishes. Carefully break 2 eggs into each and pour a bit of melted butter over the yolks. Place the ramekins in a larger dish and pour in enough hot water to go halfway up their sides. Bake for 6 to 7 minutes, just until the whites are set. Do not overbake. Sprinkle with salt and white pepper. Spoon the sauce over the eggs and serve immediately.

SERVES 2

. . . .

Peppered Beef Bacon

Beef bacon is cured beef, not really bacon at all, but less fatty and therefore more healthy.

Preheat the oven to 350°. Allow 2 or 3 slices of beef bacon per person. Sprinkle each slice liberally with coarsely cracked black pepper. Bake on a rack for 10 to 15 minutes, until crisp. Drain on paper towels and serve immediately.

BRENTWOOD PARK

. . . .

Los Angeles has been described as many suburbs in search of a city. Actually, it is many small cities, so diversified, so different from one another, that there is no need to search, only to choose.

Where one lives in Los Angeles has to do mostly with the way of life one chooses—by the sea or in a valley, in a canyon or on a hilltop, with land for a garden or water for a boat, with horses or a tennis court. Perhaps not surprisingly, having made the choice, people find themselves living with the kind of people they are. If not, they can always move.

Brentwood offers dignity, with stately homes and sweeping lawns. Its people actively support charities and the community. They travel. They know good food and how to prepare it. They live with considerable style, often with their own carefully assembled art collections.

They are also discerning enough to know that serving a Chinese buffet in a home filled with the art of eighteenth- and nineteenth-century American painters and sculptors is not incongruous. The yin-yang mystique of Chinese food is not only fascinating, but adaptable. "Rules of the stomach" is a perceptive Chinese translation of *gastronomy*, and some of the rules have seeped into California cooking. Vegetables are often stir-fried, for example, and it is Chinese thinking to combine hot meats with cold, crisp greens. They introduced us to snow peas, bean sprouts, shiitake mushrooms, the Szechuan peppercorn, and more. They taught us brevity in cooking.

The formal dinner presented at another time in this Brentwood Park home is an update of a traditional American meal, not at all as it would have been served in an earlier century. Shrimp in the pumpkin bisque is a sly California fillip. So are herbs and Cognac added to the pork, with fennel as a vegetable—which is not too usual even now, even in California, where it grows.

113

ORIENTAL COCKTAIL
RECEPTION

FOR **12** TO **16**

Curried Beef Buns • Shrimp in the Shell,
Shanghai Style

Cold Lemon Chicken

Chinese Duck with Plum Sauce in Pancakes

Stir-Fried Lima Beans • Tea Eggs

Lettuce Cups with Minced Squab, Pork, and Mushrooms

Lichees, Plums, Cherries, and Peaches

Blanc de Noir

· · · · · · · · · · · · · · · ·

Curried Beef Buns

This would be a bao if it were steamed, one of the many varieties of dim sum. The buns freeze beautifully, to be baked or steamed after defrosting.

YEAST BUNS
- 1 package active dry yeast
- ¾ cup sugar
- 1¾ cups lukewarm water (105° to 115°)
- 1 teaspoon baking powder
- 5½ to 6½ cups unbleached all-purpose flour
  Dark Oriental sesame oil

CURRIED BEEF
- 1 tablespoon peanut oil
- 1 pound lean ground beef
- 1 8-ounce can of bamboo shoots, drained and diced
- 3 tablespoons ketchup
- 1 tablespoon Chinese curry paste
- 1 tablespoon oyster sauce
- 1 teaspoon salt
- ½ teaspoon sugar
- 2 scallions, chopped

EGG WASH
- 1 egg white, beaten
- 1 teaspoon water
- ¼ teaspoon sugar

- 2 tablespoons unsalted butter, melted

To make the buns, dissolve the yeast and sugar in the warm water in a large bowl or the bowl of a heavy-duty electric mixer. Immediately add the baking powder and 4 cups flour. Mix well. Knead for 10 minutes with a dough hook or transfer to a lightly floured board and knead for 20 minutes by hand. Add more flour as needed. The dough should be elastic, smooth, and dry. Place in a greased bowl, turning once to coat the surface, cover with a damp cloth, and leave in a warm, draft-free place until the dough has doubled in volume. (This may take up to 3 hours.)

While the dough is rising, prepare the curried beef. Heat the oil in a wok or skillet. Add the beef and bamboo shoots. Stir-fry until the meat is browned; drain off the fat. Add the ketchup, curry powder, oyster sauce, salt, sugar, and scallions and stir-fry for an additional 2 minutes. Let cool and set aside.

When the dough has doubled, punch it down and knead for 5 minutes. Shape into two long cylinders about 1½ inches in diameter. Cut each cylinder into 1-inch slices. You should have about 24 pieces. Keep the dough that is not being worked covered with the damp cloth. Roll each piece of dough into a 4-inch circle, thicker in the center than at the edges. Brush with sesame oil. Hold the dough in the palm of your hand and put 1 to 2 tablespoons of the beef filling in the center. Gather up the dough around the filling by pleating it along the edges. Bring the pleats up and twist firmly to seal. Place, twisted side down, on a square of foil. Cover and allow the filled buns to rise in a warm place for 1 hour.

Preheat the oven to 350°. Combine the egg white, water, and sugar to make the egg wash. Brush over the buns. Bake for 20 to 25 minutes, until golden. Remove from the oven and brush with melted butter. Serve hot.

MAKES ABOUT 24 BUNS

. . . .

Shrimp in the Shell, Shanghai Style

Shanghai chefs seem to do better with shrimp than anyone else in China—maybe in the world. This is an excellent dish. Cooking the shrimp in the shells improves the flavor, but if you prefer, the shells can be removed before serving.

- 2½ pounds medium-size raw shrimp, with shells on
- 4 tablespoons vegetable oil
- 4 thin slices of fresh ginger
- 3 scallions, cut into quarters
- 2 tablespoons dry sherry
- 4 tablespoons dark soy sauce
- 3 tablespoons sugar
- 2 teaspoons red wine vinegar

Remove the legs of the shrimp with scissors. Make an opening in the back of each shrimp and devein, leaving the shell and tail on.

Heat the oil in a pan or wok. Stir-fry the ginger and scallions over low heat for 30 seconds, until there is an aroma. Add the shrimp and stir-fry for 1 minute over high heat. Add the remaining ingredients and stir-fry until the sauce is glazed, about 2 minutes. Serve hot or at room temperature.

SERVES 12 TO 16 AS PART OF A BUFFET

Chinese food in fine old English silver.

Cold Lemon Chicken

Red and green peppers add color and crispness to this dish, which can be made a day ahead.

- 4 **to 5 whole chicken breasts, halved, boned, and skinned**
- 8 **large dried black mushrooms**
- 2 **or 3 lemons**
- 3 **tablespoons peanut oil**
- ¼ **cup fresh ginger, cut into fine julienne**
- ⅓ **cup red and green bell peppers, cut into fine julienne**
- 2 **tablespoons sugar**
- 1 **teaspoon salt, or to taste**
- ½ **teaspoon chili paste with garlic**
- 1½ **teaspoons lemon extract**

Put the chicken breasts in a flat bowl and place the bowl on a rack in a covered steamer over boiling water. Steam for 45 minutes to 1 hour, until tender. Let cool in the juices, remove (reserve the broth), and cut the chicken into bite-size pieces. Set aside. Strain the broth, measure it, and if necessary add enough water to bring the amount to 1 cup. Set aside.

While the chicken is steaming, put the mushrooms in a small bowl and cover with boiling water. Let stand for 30 minutes, drain, squeeze dry, cut off the stems, and cut the mushrooms into fine julienne. Set aside.

With a sharp paring knife or vegetable peeler, remove the rind of 1 lemon in long shreds, being careful not to include any of the bitter pith, and cut the rind into fine julienne. Grate the rind of the second lemon. Squeeze enough lemon juice to measure ½ cup.

Heat a pan (preferably a wok) and add 3 tablespoons peanut oil. When the oil is hot, add the ginger and mushrooms and stir-fry over low heat for 30 seconds. Add the peppers and julienned lemon rind. Stir-fry for

a few seconds. Add the sugar and the reserved chicken broth. Bring to a boil and add the lemon juice and salt. Add the grated lemon rind, chili paste with garlic, and lemon extract. Add the chicken pieces and cook for 30 seconds. Transfer to a bowl and let cool to room temperature before serving.

SERVES 12 TO 16 AS PART OF A BUFFET

. . . .

Chinese Duck with Plum Sauce in Pancakes

A simplification of Peking duck, prepared for a buffet. The ducks are not difficult, but if further simplifying seems desirable, they can be found already prepared in the Chinese markets of most cities.

- 2 **4- to 5-pound ducks**
  Salt and freshly ground black pepper, to taste
- 2 **medium garlic cloves, crushed**
- 2 **small pieces of fresh ginger**
- 1 **cup coarsely chopped onion**
- 2 **celery stalks, cut into chunks**
- 1 **cup ice water**
- 1⅓ **cups plum sauce**
- ⅔ **cup bean sauce**

PANCAKES
MAKES ABOUT 16 PANCAKES
- 1½ **cups unbleached all-purpose flour**
- ¼ **teaspoon salt**
- 2 **eggs, beaten**
- 1½ **cups milk**
- 1 **cup water**

  Additional plum sauce
  Very thin slices of cucumber

GARNISH
  Scallion brushes (see Note)

Preheat the oven to 400°. Pat the ducks inside and out with paper towels. Rub the skin and cavities with salt and pepper, garlic, and ginger. Stuff the cavities with the onion and celery, and any remaining garlic and ginger. Place the ducks, breast side up, on a rack in a shallow pan and roast for 20 minutes, pricking the skin frequently to let the fat drain off. Remove the roasting pan from the oven and lift the ducks out one at a time. Put the ducks on a wire rack or in a colander in the sink and carefully pour ice water over them. This crisps the skin. Return the ducks to the pan, breast side up, and roast for another 20 minutes.

While the ducks are roasting, combine the plum and bean sauces. After the second 20 minutes of roasting, remove the ducks from the oven, turn them, and brush some of the plum-bean sauce over the backs. Return them to the oven, breast side down, for 15 minutes. Turn the ducks breast side up again, brush with more sauce, and roast for another 30 minutes (about 1 hour 25 minutes in all), basting occasionally. Let cool. Reserve the rest of the basting sauce.

To make the pancakes, sift the flour and salt into a mixing bowl. Combine the eggs, milk, and water. Add to the dry ingredients and beat until smooth. Cover lightly and let stand for 30 to 60 minutes.

To cook, lightly oil a 6- or 7-inch skillet (preferably nonstick) and place over low heat. Stir the batter and, off the heat, pour a small amount into the skillet. Rotate the pan to cover the bottom with batter, and pour out any excess. Cook until set but not browned. Turn and cook the other side. Remove and let cool on a clean towel. Continue until all the batter is cooked, brushing the skillet with oil as necessary.

Cut the ducks in half lengthwise with poultry shears. Remove the legs and reserve whole; discard the wings. Remove all meat from the carcass and slice the meat. Brush the legs, meat, and pancakes with the reserved basting sauce. Wrap a few slices of meat and cucumber inside each pancake and fold over. Arrange the pancakes and legs on a platter. Garnish with scallion brushes. Serve at room temperature.

NOTE: To make scallion brushes, cut each scallion into a 3-inch piece. Trim off the root. With a sharp paring knife, make a 1-inch-deep cut through the root end, then make another cut perpendicular to the first one. Make 2 more cuts in the same manner so that you have 8 pie-shaped wedges. Put the scallions into ice water so that the ends will curl.

SERVES 12 TO 16 AS PART OF A BUFFET

Tea eggs, like elegant marble.

Stir-Fried Lima Beans

The un-Chinese lima bean responds nicely to a simple stir-fry. This dish can be made a day ahead, refrigerated, and brought back to room temperature.

- **3 tablespoons peanut oil**
- **2 10-ounce packages of frozen baby lima beans, defrosted and well dried**
- **2 teaspoons salt**
- **2 tablespoons sugar**
- **½ cup chicken stock, preferably homemade (page 17)**
- **2 teaspoons dark Oriental sesame oil**

Heat a pan or wok over high heat and add the oil. Heat for 30 seconds. Add the beans and stir-fry quickly for 2 minutes. Add the salt and sugar and toss for 30 seconds. Add the stock, stir, and reduce the heat to low. Cover and simmer for 5 minutes.

Remove the cover, turn up the heat, and stir-fry for 1 minute. Add the sesame oil and stir for 30 seconds. Transfer to a serving dish and let cool. Serve at room temperature.

SERVES 12 TO 16 AS PART OF A BUFFET

. . . .

Tea Eggs

The eggs come out patterned with spidery brown lines, permeated with the musky flavor of the tea.

- **16 eggs**
- **4 tablespoons salt**
- **4 tablespoons soy sauce**
- **2 or 3 whole star anise**
- **¼ cup black tea leaves**

Put the eggs in a saucepan, cover with cold water, and bring to a boil. Reduce the heat and simmer for 15 to 20 minutes. Pour off the hot water, add cold water to the pan, and let the eggs cool for 30 minutes, then drain. Do not peel, but crack the eggs all over with the back of a spoon or by rolling them on a flat surface.

Put the cracked eggs back in the pan, cover with fresh cold water, and bring to a boil. Add the rest of the ingredients, reduce the heat, and simmer, covered, for 1½ hours. Remove from the heat, let cool, cover, and store in the liquid in the refrigerator. To serve, drain, remove the shells, and put the eggs in a serving bowl.

SERVES 12 TO 16 AS PART OF A BUFFET

**Clockwise from top:
Duck in pancake with
plum sauce; curried beef
bun; lettuce cups with
minced squab, pork, and
mushrooms; cold lemon
chicken.**

Lettuce Cups with Minced Squab, Pork, and Mushrooms

A dish to please even those who don't like Chinese food. In spite of a fair amount of chopping, it is simple to prepare. Be a littly chary with the amount of filling so they will be easy to handle.

3	1-pound squabs or 3 whole chicken breasts
½	pound ground lean pork
1	tablespoon dry sherry
1	tablespoon light soy sauce
1	tablespoon dark soy sauce
	Freshly ground black pepper, to taste
1	egg
4	dried black mushrooms
½	teaspoon salt
2	tablespoons oyster sauce
½	teaspoon sugar
1	teaspoon dark Oriental sesame oil
1	teaspoon chili paste with garlic
4	tablespoons (approximately) peanut oil
1	large garlic clove, minced
1	tablespoon fresh ginger, minced
⅔	cup minced bamboo shoots
⅔	cup minced water chestnuts
½	cup peeled and minced carrots
4	scallions, minced
1½	teaspoons cornstarch dissolved in 1 tablespoon water (optional)
12	to 16 small iceberg lettuce leaves

Remove the meat from the squabs or chicken breasts and dice fine. Combine with the pork. Make a marinade of the sherry, soy sauces, pepper, and egg and combine with the squab-pork mixture. Let stand for 30 to 60 minutes.

Meanwhile, soak the mushrooms in boiling water for 30 minutes. Drain, squeeze dry, remove the stems, and mince. Set aside. Combine the salt, oyster sauce, sugar, sesame oil, and chili paste and set aside.

Heat a skillet or wok and add 2 tablespoons peanut oil. Over very low heat fry the garlic and ginger for 30 seconds. Add the squab-pork mixture and stir-fry until the meat changes color. Remove. Add the remaining 2 tablespoons oil to the pan and stir-fry the mushrooms, bamboo shoots, water chestnuts, carrots, and scallions for 1 minute. Return the squab-pork mixture to the pan. Add the oyster sauce mixture and combine well. Add the cornstarch paste if the filling is too watery. To serve, wrap the minced squab mixture in individual lettuce leaves and have guests eat with their fingers.

SERVES 12 TO 16 AS PART OF A BUFFET

FORMAL DINNER

FOR 10

Pumpkin-Shrimp Bisque

Pork Loin Braised in Milk • **W**ehani Rice

Cranberry Relish with Pears, Apples, and Grand Marnier

Braised Fennel with Goat Cheese

Four-Leaf Salad with Lemon-Mint Vinaigrette

Persimmon Pudding with Hard Sauce

WINES:

Chardonnay with Soup

Merlot with Dinner

Late-Harvest Gewurztraminer with Dessert

· · · · · · · · · · ·

Pumpkin-Shrimp Bisque

Pumpkin soup becomes a new experience when shrimp is added to the traditional ingredients.

- 6 tablespoons (¾ stick) unsalted butter
- 1 large onion, diced
- 1 cup finely chopped leeks (white part only)
- 2 16-ounce cans of puréed pumpkin
- 6 to 7 cups chicken stock, preferably homemade (page 17)
- ½ cup minced fresh parsley
- 3 cups milk
- Salt and freshly ground white pepper, to taste
- Freshly ground nutmeg, to taste
- 1 pound raw shrimp, peeled and deveined
- 1 tablespoon freshly squeezed lemon juice

GARNISH
- 10 medium-size cooked shrimp
- Parsley, preferably the flat-leaf variety

In a large pot, melt the butter. Sauté the onion and leeks for 8 to 10 minutes, until soft and golden. Stir in the pumpkin. Add 6 cups chicken stock and the minced parsley. Simmer over low heat for 15 to 20 minutes. Stir in the milk. Add the salt, pepper, and nutmeg and simmer for 10 minutes. (Do not boil.)

Coarsely chop half the shrimp and set aside. Add the remaining whole shrimp to the soup and cook for 2 to 3 minutes, just until they turn pink. Transfer the solids to a food processor fitted with the steel blade, add about ¾ cup of the liquid, and purée until smooth. Stir in the lemon juice. Return the purée to the pot, and cook gently for 5 to 10 minutes. Taste for seasonings and add more chicken stock to thin the soup, if necessary. Add the reserved chopped shrimp and cook for 1 to 2 minutes more, just until they turn pink. Ladle into heated bowls. If desired, garnish with a single shrimp and a sprig of parsley.

SERVES 10

Pork Loin Braised in Milk

The loin is the best cut of pork. Cooking in milk results in a rich and succulent crust, enhanced by the herb-scented sauce.

- 1 5-pound center-cut pork loin roast, trimmed of fat
- 3 medium garlic cloves, slivered
- Salt and freshly ground white pepper, to taste
- Vegetable oil
- 1 large onion, chopped
- 1 tablespoon finely minced fresh thyme
- 1 tablespoon finely minced fresh rosemary
- 1 bay leaf
- 2 to 3 quarts milk
- 1 tablespoon Cognac or brandy

With a small sharp paring knife make several holes in the pork and insert the garlic slivers. Season the meat with salt and pepper. Preheat the oven to 375°.

Brown the roast on all sides in a little vegetable oil. Set aside. In another pan, sauté the onion in a little oil for 8 to 10 minutes, until softened and golden. Add 1½ teaspoons each thyme and rosemary and the bay leaf. Put the onion mixture in the bottom of a flameproof pan just large enough to hold the roast. Place the meat on top. Heat enough milk to cover the roast at least halfway up, and add a little salt to the milk. When the milk has reached a boil, pour it over the meat. Bring it back to a boil.

Place the roast, uncovered, in the oven and cook for about 2½ hours. Turn the meat over, being careful not to break the crust, and cook for another ½ hour, or until the internal temperature reaches 160°. Take the pan out of the oven, remove the roast, and keep it warm.

Strain the sauce and in a wide pan, over medium high heat, reduce it to 2 cups. Add the remaining 1½ teaspoons each thyme and rosemary and the Cognac or brandy. Season with salt and pepper, if desired. Slice the meat and overlap the slices on a serving tray. Pass the sauce separately.

SERVES 10

The bisque is garnished with whole shrimp and flat-leaf parsley.

Still-life of food and still-life of flowers.

Wehani Rice

Grown in Northern California, Wehani rice is crunchy, with a slightly nutty flavor. It may not be available everywhere; wild rice or brown rice can be substituted.

- 4 cups chicken stock, preferably homemade (page 17)
  Salt, to taste
- 2 cups Wehani rice (or wild rice)
- 6 tablespoons (¾ stick) unsalted butter
- ½ cup thinly sliced (on the diagonal) scallions
- 1 cup toasted pecans, chopped

Bring the chicken stock to a boil, and add salt if the stock is unsalted. Stir in the rice and return to a boil. Reduce the heat and cover with a tight-fitting lid. Cook for 45 to 55 minutes, until the rice is tender. Pour off any excess liquid.

While the rice is cooking, melt the butter in a skillet and add the scallions. Sauté lightly. Stir in the cooked rice and toasted pecans. Serve immediately.

SERVES 10

· · · · · · · · · · · · ·

Cranberry Relish with Pears, Apples, and Grand Marnier

Cranberries and apples make a fresh-tasting variation on both the applesauce usual with pork and the cranberry sauce traditional for holidays. Since cranberries are available only briefly in the late fall, it's a good idea to freeze a bag or two for year-round use.

- 3 tart apples, such as Granny Smith or Pippin, peeled, cored, and diced
- 2 slightly ripe pears, peeled, cored, and diced
- 2 pounds fresh cranberries
- 1 cup golden raisins
- 2 cups sugar
- 1 cup freshly squeezed orange juice
- 2 tablespoons grated orange rind
- 2 teaspoons cinnamon
- ¼ teaspoon nutmeg
- ½ cup Grand Marnier or other orange liqueur

Mix together all the ingredients except the Grand Marnier in a saucepan. Bring to a boil, reduce the heat, and simmer, uncovered, for 45 minutes, until thick. Stir in the Grand Marnier, let cool to room temperature, and refrigerate, covered, until serving time.

MAKES 6 CUPS

· · · · · · · · · · · · ·

Braised Fennel with Goat Cheese

The best fennel is the Florentine variety (finnochio in Italy) with the fat bottom. It is lovely as a braised vegetable, and is also fine raw, in a salad or as a crudité.

- 4 to 5 fennel bulbs
- 9 tablespoons unsalted butter
- 1½ cups chicken stock, preferably homemade (page 17)
  Salt and freshly ground black pepper, to taste
  Olive oil
- 8 ounces goat cheese
  Chopped fresh parsley

Preheat the oven to 400°. Cut off the top and bottom of each fennel bulb and discard any tough outer leaves. Cut each bulb vertically into slices about ¾ inch thick.

Melt the butter in a shallow flameproof pan and add the chicken stock. Put the fennel in a single layer in the pan and add salt and pepper. Place on top of the stove and bring to a boil. Cover tightly and put in the oven for 20 to 25 minutes, until the fennel is tender but still firm. Drain off the stock, and turn the fennel slices over. Brush with olive oil. Crumble on the goat cheese, and return the pan to the oven for 5 to 6 minutes, until the cheese is bubbly. Serve immediately, sprinkled with parsley.

VARIATION: Sliced mozzarella and freshly grated Parmesan may be substituted for the goat cheese.

SERVES 10

The main course is served on elegant gold-rimmed plates.

A cool-looking four-leaf salad garnished with lemon zest.

Four-Leaf Salad with Lemon-Mint Vinaigrette

A refreshing taste after the richness of the pork. For a formal dinner such as this, it should be served last, as a separate course.

½ small head of red leaf lettuce
1 medium head of Boston lettuce
½ bunch of spinach, stems removed
½ small head of curly endive

LEMON-MINT VINAIGRETTE
⅔ cup Champagne vinegar
1 teaspoon finely grated lemon rind
2 tablespoons chopped fresh mint leaves
1 teaspoon salt
   Freshly ground black pepper, to taste
1⅓ cups extra virgin olive oil

GARNISH
   Lemon zest

Wash and dry the lettuces, spinach, and curly endive. Tear into bite-size pieces and combine in a large salad bowl.

To make the vinaigrette, combine the vinegar with the grated lemon rind, mint, salt, and pepper. Slowly whisk in the olive oil until well combined.

Just before serving, toss the salad with enough dressing to coat and garnish with lemon zest.

SERVES 10

. . . .

Persimmon Pudding with Hard Sauce

An old-fashioned favorite made festive with dates, pecans, and a variation of the traditional hard sauce.

   Approximately 6 very ripe persimmons
   (see Note)
1½ cups sugar
4½ tablespoons unsalted butter, melted
¾ teaspoon salt
1½ teaspoons cinnamon
¾ teaspoon freshly grated nutmeg
   Scant ½ teaspoon ground cloves
1½ cups unbleached all-purpose flour
1 tablespoon baking soda
¾ cup milk
1½ cups chopped pitted dates
1½ cups chopped pecans

Coffee and dessert are ready to serve.

GARNISH
   Crystallized mint leaves and crystallized violets (available at specialty stores and some supermarkets)

HARD SAUCE
8 tablespoons (1 stick) unsalted butter, at room temperature
1 cup light brown sugar
1 egg, well beaten
1 cup heavy cream

Slice the persimmons in half. Remove any seeds and strings, and scoop out the pulp, being careful not to scrape too close to the skin. Purée until smooth in a food processor fitted with the steel blade. You should have 2½ cups of pulp.

Preheat the oven to 350°. Grease a 9-inch springform, tube pan, or other ovenproof mold and set aside.

Combine the pulp with the rest of the pudding ingredients in the order given and pour into the pan. Cover tightly with foil. Bake for approximately 1 hour 15 minutes. When the pudding is done, the outside will pull away from the mold. Let cool slightly and invert onto a serving plate. Garnish with crystallized mint leaves and violets, if desired.

To make the hard sauce, cream together the butter and sugar. Beat in the egg and cook over hot water until the mixture thickens. Remove from the heat and let cool. Whip the cream to soft peaks and fold it into the hard sauce just before serving. The pudding may be served hot or cold, with the sauce on the side.

NOTE: Persimmons are available for only a short time in the fall. However, the pulp freezes beautifully.

VARIATION: The pudding may also be steamed. Pour the mixture into a greased mold, cover tightly, and place on a rack in a large pot with a tight lid. Fill the pot with enough water to go halfway up the sides of the mold. Bring the water to a boil, reduce the heat to a simmer, and steam the pudding for 2 to 2½ hours.

SERVES 10 OR MORE

MANDEVILLE CANYON

. . . .

Mandeville Canyon is rural surrounded by urban. Its people live in large, low-slung, rambling California ranch houses with room between the canyon walls for swimming pools, hot tubs, and even horses. Probably no where else in the world is country living so close to city living. A working day can include a ride into the mountains, a swim, dinner in a good restaurant, a play or a concert. It is a luxuriously informal life, zestful but also purposeful. These canyonites work hard, play hard, and enjoy. They are quick to fight for causes they believe in, such as fending off developers in the Santa Monica mountains.

It was particularly suitable that these enjoyers of life chose the food of those other enjoyers, the Italians, for this menu. Lamb is eaten in many parts of Italy, often spit-roasted—especially if it is very young. It is variously seasoned, with olive oil, anchovies, capers, sometimes only with salt, pepper, and vinegar. Here, a butterflied leg, quickly cooked over charcoal and mesquite, is right in the spirit. Mesquite, a legume found in the Southwest and Mexico, burns with a crisp, sagey fragrance and is currently the fuel of choice for California-style grilling. Applewood, grape cuttings, and *kiawe* from Hawaii are recent contenders too.

Eggplant can also be attributed to Italy, although more to the south, where the influence of the Arabs was stronger; Sicily is particularly proud of its *caponata*. In the north, it is mostly found with the antipasto. Risotto has been called the ''great paladin of Italian cooking'' and, with white truffles, ''God's great porridge.'' In Italy there are more versions of risotto than can be counted. Almost anything fresh and in season could be added to the preparation of the rice.

EVENING BARBECUE

FOR **8**

Smoky Roasted Eggplant with
Tomatoes and Goat Cheese

Butterflied Leg of Lamb with Juniper Berries
and Rosemary

Risotto Rusticano   •   **F**ocaccia

Hearty Zinfandel

Tiramisu   •   **E**spresso

**The table is set in a
shaded shelter beside the
pool.**

Everything is ready on handmade, unglazed platters.

Smoky Roasted Eggplant with Tomatoes and Goat Cheese

An excellent, simple preparation for eggplant. Balsamic vinegar makes the dressing distinctive.

> 8 **Japanese eggplants**
> **Olive oil**
> 1 **bunch of chives, minced**
> ¾ **pound goat cheese, cut into ½-inch pieces**

BALSAMIC DRESSING
> 2 **tablespoons balsamic vinegar**
> ½ **cup extra virgin olive oil**
> **Salt and freshly ground black pepper, to taste**
>
> **Red leaf and Boston lettuce leaves, or other greens**
> 4 **large tomatoes, peeled and quartered**
> **Salt and freshly ground black pepper, to taste**

Prepare coals for a barbecue or heat a grill. Cut the eggplants lengthwise into slices about ½ inch thick, keeping them attached at the stem end. Brush with olive oil and barbecue or grill for 6 to 8 minutes (turning once), until grid marks appear and the eggplant is softened. Set aside.

Press some of the chives onto each slice of goat cheese and set aside. Make the dressing by whisking the vinegar and oil together in a small bowl. Add the salt and pepper.

Line a large platter with lettuce leaves. Arrange the eggplant, goat cheese slices, and tomatoes separately on the platter. Season with salt and pepper, and drizzle on the dressing. Serve at room temperature.

SERVES 8

Butterflied Leg of Lamb with Juniper Berries and Rosemary

A splendid way to prepare lamb. Juniper berries, which are dry when ripe, can be found on the spice counters of most supermarkets. Fresh rosemary also is usually available. Throw a little on the burning coals for extra flavor.

> 1 **6- to 8-pound leg of lamb, butterflied (see Note)**
> **Olive oil**
> 1 **teaspoon coarse salt**
> ⅓ **cup juniper berries**
> 2 **teaspoons black peppercorns**
> 3 **tablespoons fresh rosemary or 1 tablespoon dried**

Rub the lamb with olive oil to coat and sprinkle with the salt. Crush the juniper berries and peppercorns with the back of a heavy saucepan or in a spice grinder. Combine with the rosemary and press into the lamb, turning to coat thoroughly. Refrigerate for 4 to 6 hours.

Cook on a very hot barbecue grill, turning once or twice, for 30 to 40 minutes, until the meat registers 130° to 135° on an instant-read thermometer. The meat should be crusty on the outside and pink inside. Let sit for 15 minutes before carving. Cut against the grain into thin diagonal slices and serve with its own juices.

NOTE: If desired, have the butcher pound the thicker portions of the lamb so that all of the meat will be the same thickness and will cook more evenly.

SERVES 8

Risotto Rusticano

This recipe is flexible in everything but the rice and its preparation. Vegetables can be varied according to season and availability. The same vegetables would also make a marvelous pasta primavera.

- ¼ **pound asparagus, peeled and sliced diagonally into ½-inch pieces**
- ¼ **pound zucchini, sliced diagonally into ⅛-inch-thick slices**
- ¼ **pound yellow summer squash, sliced diagonally into ¼-inch-thick slices**
- ¼ **pound tender young green beans or haricots verts, trimmed and cut diagonally into 2-inch pieces**
- ¼ **pound sugar snap peas, cut in half (optional)**
- 8 **tablespoons (1 stick) unsalted butter**
- 12 **cherry tomatoes, stems removed**
- 1 **red bell pepper, halved, seeded, and cut into ½-inch squares**
- 1 **yellow bell pepper, halved, seeded, and cut into ½-inch squares (optional)**
- ¼ **pound mushrooms, thinly sliced**
- 5 **cups chicken stock (approximately), preferably homemade (page 17)**
- ¼ **cup olive oil**
- ¾ **cup finely chopped onion**
- 1 **large garlic clove, finely chopped**
- 2½ **cups Italian arborio rice (available in Italian markets and some supermarkets)**
- ⅓ **cup dry white wine**
- ⅓ **cup freshly grated Parmesan cheese, plus additional cheese for passing**
- ⅓ **cup chopped fresh parsley (preferably the flat-leaf Italian type)**

Cook the asparagus in a large pot of boiling salted water just until crisp-tender. Remove with a slotted spoon and immediately rinse under cold water to stop the cooking. Drain well, dry, and set aside. In the same pot of boiling water, separately cook the zucchini, summer squash, green beans, and sugar snap peas (if used) in the same manner. Heat 4 tablespoons of butter in a skillet and quickly sauté the cherry tomatoes, peppers, and mushrooms. Set aside.

Heat the chicken stock to a simmer. In a large heavy saucepan heat the olive oil and, over medium high heat, sauté the onion and garlic until softened and golden. Add the rice and cook for 1 minute, stirring to combine. Add the wine and stir until evaporated. Add ⅓ cup of the simmering stock and stir until the rice absorbs the liquid. Add another ⅓ cup of stock, cooking and stirring until the rice has again absorbed the liquid. Continue adding stock ⅓ cup at a time, making sure to loosen the rice from the bottom of the pan to prevent its sticking. Regulate the heat so that the total cooking time is about 20 minutes. As the rice cooks the stock will be absorbed at a slower rate.

After 15 minutes, when the rice is almost done, add the vegetables. Stirring gently to avoid bruising the vegetables, continue to cook, adding stock until the rice is tender but firm to the bite and creamy. The vegetables should retain their identity. You may not need to use all of the stock.

Remove from the heat and add the remaining butter, stirring to melt. Stir in the Parmesan cheese, transfer to a serving plate, sprinkle with parsley, and serve at once. Pass additional Parmesan cheese.

SERVES 8 OR MORE

. . . .

Focaccia (Italian Flat Bread)

Focaccia is a civilized version of hearth bread, so ancient that no one knows where it originated—perhaps the mother of all breads.

- 2 **packages active dry yeast**
- 1 **teaspoon sugar**
- 1¾ **cups lukewarm water (105° to 115°)**
- ⅓ **cup extra virgin olive oil, plus extra to drizzle on the bread**
- 1½ **teaspoons salt**
- 4 **to 5½ cups unbleached all-purpose flour**
  Coarse salt

Dissolve the yeast and sugar in 1 cup lukewarm water in a bowl and let sit until foamy. In another bowl, add the remaining ¾ cup water, the olive oil, and the salt. Pour in the yeast mixture. Blend in the flour, 1 cup at a time, until the dough comes together. Knead on a floured board for 10 minutes, adding flour as needed to make it smooth and elastic. Put the dough in an oiled bowl, turn to coat well, and cover with a towel. Let rise in a warm draft-free place for 1 hour, until doubled.

Punch down the dough, knead it for about 5 minutes, and gently roll it out to fit a jelly roll pan, 15½ inches × 10½ inches. Let rise for 15 minutes, covered. Oil your fingers and make impressions with them in the dough, 1 inch apart. Let rise for 1 hour.

Preheat the oven to 400°. Drizzle the dough with olive oil and sprinkle with coarse salt. Bake for 15 to 20 minutes, until golden brown. Sprinkle with additional oil if desired. Cut into squares and serve warm.

MAKES 1 FLAT BREAD

A bounty of fruit and
vegetables serve as the
centerpiece, with more
bounty on the terra cotta
plates.

Tiramisu

An adaptation of a rich dessert originating in Milan, using cream cheese instead of mascarpone, and very pretty in a glass bowl. Serve with cups of espresso.

- 6 **egg yolks**
- 1 **cup sugar**
- ½ **cup sweet Marsala wine**
- 3 **8-ounce packages cream cheese, at room temperature, cut into pieces**
- 1½ **cups freshly brewed espresso or other strong coffee, at room temperature**
- ½ **cup Kahlua liqueur**
- 1 **to 2 packages Italian ladyfingers or champagne biscuits (available at Italian markets and gourmet shops)**

GARNISH
- 1 **cup heavy cream, whipped and lightly sweetened**
  Shaved semisweet chocolate

Put the egg yolks in the bowl of an electric mixer. Add the sugar and mix until light and fluffy. Add the Marsala and mix well. Slowly add the cream cheese, a piece at a time, until the mixture is thick and creamy.

Combine the espresso and Kahlua in a bowl and quickly dip the ladyfingers, one at a time, into this mixture. Line 8 individual glass dessert dishes or wine goblets with the ladyfingers and spoon in the cream cheese mixture. Refrigerate until ready to serve.

Just before serving, decorate the tiramisu with whipped cream piped through the star tube of a pastry bag. Scatter chocolate shavings over the top.

NOTE: This dessert may also be made in a large glass serving bowl. Layer the ladyfingers alternately with the cream cheese mixture and decorate as above.

SERVES 8

The tiramisu is handsomely presented in old bistro compotes (right). After dark, flickering citronella candles outline the pool (above), and lights cast romantic shadows on the trees.

BEVERLY HILLS

Hollywood is a legend. Although it still exists as an industry, it does not exist in a place called Hollywood. There is a place called Hollywood, but it is another place. The Garden of Allah is a bank. Betty Grable no longer waits for Jimmy from Iowa on the corner of Hollywood and Vine. Stars are seen on Hollywood Boulevard only as names in the sidewalk, or footprints at Grauman's (now Mann's) Chinese, or, once a year, waving from open cars in the Christmas parade.

Hollywood is in Malibu or Burbank or Venice or Brentwood. In a sense, all of Los Angeles is now Hollywood, which is no longer a place but a state of mind, and not at all what the rest of the world considers to be either Hollywood or Los Angeles.

So this formal, black-tie "Hollywood" dinner took place in Beverly Hills. The occasion was a gathering of friends to celebrate after the Academy Awards. The dinner had all the expected showmanship—black plates set on a camel-colored table with outsize purple onion flowers in black vases, and place cards wearing black bow ties. The award-winning work of the hostess, a Hollywood photographer, was white on black. For the first course, the best black caviar was tied into pale crêpes and served on the black plates.

The rest of the dinner, however, was politely restrained, contemporary thinking. There were no blatant challenges, no astonishing combinations. What could be more simply elegant than a veal medallion with turnip gratin and sweet, crisp, brightly colored baby vegetables? A chocolate-pear tart was an appropriate finale.

Sunday brunch following a glittering late night is a good custom, entirely suited to Hollywood, where, of course, Sundays are always sunny.

BLACK-TIE DINNER

FOR 6

Caviar Pouches

Veal Medallions with Onion Marmalade

Mixed Baby Vegetables

Gratin of Turnips

Chocolate-Pear Tart

WINES:

Brut or Nature Sparkling with Caviar Pouches

Chardonnay with Veal

Apricot Wine with the Tart

. . . .

The table setting of black, silver, and gold complements Ellen Graham's photographs of Holly-wood celebrities. The stark simplicity of black plates dramatizes the first course (above) and main course (right).

Caviar Pouches

Also called "beggar's purses," these are an elaboration, one must suppose, of the Russian blini. It is easier with two people to do the pouches, one to hold and one to tie. Use good-quality caviar; it will go a long way.

2 eggs
Large pinch of salt
½ cup unbleached all-purpose flour
¼ cup cake flour
1 cup less 2 tablespoons milk
2 tablespoons unsalted butter, melted
1 tablespoon beer
Peanut oil
3 bunches of chives (or more, depending on length)
8 ounces crème fraîche, well chilled (see Note, page 53)
4 ounces black caviar

In the bowl of an electric mixer, blend the eggs with the salt and mix in the flours. Gradually add the milk, blending well. Mix in the butter and beer. Let the batter sit at room temperature for 30 minutes.

Brush the bottom of a small crêpe pan or other nonstick pan with peanut oil. Set over moderately high heat until the oil is just beginning to smoke. Off the heat, pour in a small amount of batter. Quickly tilt the pan in all directions so that the batter forms a thin crêpe about 4½ inches in diameter. Return the pan to the heat. When the crêpe is set, lift the edges with a spatula and turn to cook the other side for about 30 seconds, until spotted brown. Continue until all the batter is used. Crêpes may be refrigerated or frozen between sheets of wax paper until needed.

Quickly blanch the chives in boiling water until they are limp and refresh under cool running water. Handle gently. Dry well and reserve. Spread out several crêpes at a time and spoon a dollop of crème fraîche onto the spotty side of each. Top with a teaspoon of caviar.

Gather up the edges of each crêpe to form a pouch. Tie up each with a chive, finished in a knot or bow. If the chives are not long enough, tie 2 of them together. As they are finished, place the pouches on an oiled baking sheet. Preheat the oven to 450°. Heat the pouches for 2 to 3 minutes. Put 3 pouches on each serving plate and serve hot as a first course.

MAKES 20 TO 24 POUCHES

Veal Medallions with Onion Marmalade

Onions become almost their own marmalade when melted with stock and vinegar. The cream becomes a liaison with the veal, and the port in a light sauce subtly echoes the sweetness of the onions. This is Wolfgang Puck's special recipe.

- 3 large onions, cut into eighths
- 1 teaspoon salt, or to taste
  Freshly ground black pepper
- 3 cups chicken stock, preferably homemade (page 17)
- 1½ tablespoons sherry vinegar or red wine vinegar
- 1½ cups heavy cream
- 2 to 2½ pounds veal loin, trimmed of all fat and cut into 12 equal-size medallions
- 1½ tablespoons unbleached all-purpose flour
- 3½ tablespoons unsalted butter
- 1½ tablespoons safflower oil
- ¾ cup port

GARNISH
  Watercress or fresh herbs

Season the onions with ½ teaspoon salt and pepper to taste. In a medium saucepan, combine 2 cups of chicken stock, the vinegar, and the onions. Cook, covered, over moderate heat for 15 minutes, until the liquid is evaporated.

In a small saucepan, bring the cream to a boil and quickly reduce it to 4 or 5 tablespoons. Add the cream to the onions and bring back to a boil. Adjust the seasonings. Remove from the heat and keep warm.

Season the veal with the remaining ½ teaspoon salt and pepper to taste, and dust with the flour. Heat a large skillet and add 1½ tablespoons butter and the oil. Sauté the veal in two batches for 3 to 4 minutes on each side, until golden brown but still pink inside. Transfer to a platter and keep warm.

Pour off any grease remaining in the skillet and add the port. Over medium heat deglaze the pan by scraping up the brown bits on the bottom with a wooden spoon. Add the remaining 1 cup chicken stock, bring to a boil, and reduce to 4 to 5 tablespoons. Slowly whisk in the remaining 2 tablespoons butter.

To serve, gently heat the onions and put some on each plate. Top with 2 veal medallions and spoon on some of the sauce. Garnish with watercress or fresh herbs.

SERVES 6

Mixed Baby Vegetables

For this meal we used fiddlehead greens (the tips of young ferns) and baby corn, carrots, beets, turnips, and pattypan squash, allowing 1 of each per person.

Leaving a little of the stem on, peel the turnips and carrots, and scrub the unpeeled beets. In a pot of boiling salted water, blanch each vegetable separately, until crisp-tender. (The beets should be cooked for 5 to 10 minutes, depending on size, and then peeled.) Refresh under cold water, drain, and dry well.

Just before serving, melt unsalted butter in a shallow pan, add all the vegetables except the beets, and gently toss for about 2 minutes, just until warmed through (the beets should be sautéed separately). Season with salt and pepper and serve immediately.

A colorful tumble of baby vegetables.

Gratin of Turnips

A lovely, delicate treatment of the turnip, excellent with the veal. This would be a good accompaniment to other meats and fowl as well.

- 2 pounds turnips, peeled and quartered
- 2 cups fresh bread crumbs
- 8 tablespoons (1 stick) unsalted butter, melted
- 4 eggs, slightly beaten
- 2 teaspoons salt
- ¼ teaspoon freshly ground white pepper

Cook the turnips in boiling salted water for 20 minutes until very soft (see Note). Mash well by hand. Preheat the oven to 350° and grease a 1½-quart soufflé dish.

Mix together the mashed turnips, bread crumbs, melted butter, eggs, salt, and pepper. Spoon into the prepared dish and bake, covered, for 45 minutes. Remove the cover and bake for 15 minutes more, until golden.

NOTE: If using winter turnips, blanch them before cooking to remove their strong taste. Put the turnips in a saucepan with salted water to cover by 2 inches and boil for 3 to 5 minutes, until partially tender. Then drain and cook as above.

SERVES 8

. . . .

Chocolate-Pear Tart

A dramatic dessert, suitable for any special occasion, combines two of our true loves—fresh fruit and chocolate—most happily.

SHORTBREAD CRUST
9 tablespoons unsalted butter
9 tablespoons sifted confectioners' sugar
1½ cups sifted unbleached all-purpose flour

CHOCOLATE LAYER
6 ounces semisweet or bittersweet chocolate
2 tablespoons unsalted butter

POACHED PEARS
2 cups water
1 cup sugar
1 1-inch piece of vanilla bean (or 1
   teaspoon vanilla extract)
1 3-inch strip of lemon peel
½ cinnamon stick
   Splash of Cognac
4 pears (preferably Bosc), peeled, halved,
   stemmed, and cored

GLAZE
1 12-ounce jar of apricot preserves
2 tablespoons curaçao or other orange
   liqueur, or pear brandy

GARNISH
¼ cup sliced almonds, toasted

Preheat the oven to 350°.

To make the shortbread crust, cream together the butter and sugar. Blend in the flour to make a soft dough. Add 1 more tablespoon butter if the mixture will not incorporate all the flour.

Pat the dough evenly by hand into the bottom and 1½ to 2 inches up the sides of a 10-inch springform pan. Prick well with a fork. Bake for 12 to 15 minutes, until golden brown. Let cool completely.

Melt the chocolate and butter in a double boiler over simmering water. Spread on the bottom and sides of the tart shell and let cool until the chocolate hardens.

To prepare the poached pears, bring the water and sugar to a boil over medium heat in a large saucepan, stirring only until the sugar is dissolved. Add the vanilla bean, lemon peel, cinnamon stick, and Cognac and cook for 5 minutes. Add the pears and poach for 10 to 15 minutes, until they can be easily pierced with a sharp paring knife. Let cool in the syrup.

For the glaze, put the apricot preserves in a food processor fitted with the steel blade and process until smooth. Strain and add the liqueur.

To assemble, drain the pears well, pat them dry, cut crosswise into ¼-inch slices, and arrange carefully in the tart shell. Brush the pears with some of the apricot glaze and sprinkle with the toasted almonds.

MAKES ONE 10-INCH TART

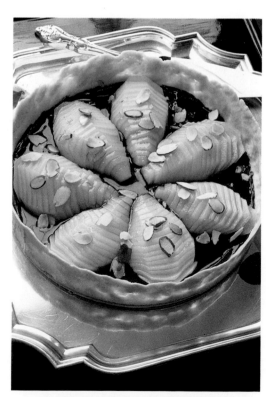

A rich pear tart in a shortbread crust.

POOLSIDE BRUNCH

FOR 12

Iced Cantaloupe Soup

Cider-Glazed Ham

Sweet Potato Chips

Layered Omelet

Blackberry Muffins

Freshly Squeezed Orange Juice

Rosé of Cabernet

Freshly Brewed Coffee

Lemons picked from the garden complement the delicate color of the soup (above). The layered omelet makes an impressive centerpiece for the brunch (right).

Iced Cantaloupe Soup

A pretty and refreshing soup that is best served well chilled. Cardamom adds an unusual flavor.

6 **small cantaloupes**
3 **tablespoons freshly squeezed lime juice**
6 **tablespoons Grand Marnier or Cointreau**
6 **tablespoons heavy cream**
   Seeds from 6 cardamom pods, freshly ground, or ¼ teaspoon ground cardamom
1 **scant teaspoon freshly grated nutmeg, or to taste**
   Large pinch of sugar

GARNISH
   Thin slices of lime or fine strips of fresh mint

Halve the cantaloupes and remove the seeds and rind. Purée the flesh until very smooth in a food processor fitted with the steel blade. Pour the purée into a bowl. You should have about 12 cups. Add the remaining ingredients and chill overnight to blend the flavors. Adjust the seasonings.

Before serving, put the soup in the freezer for about 30 minutes to chill thoroughly. Serve in chilled bowls. If desired, garnish with lime slices or mint.

SERVES 12

. . . .

Cider-Glazed Ham

This is the traditional method of roasting ham. Its success will depend on the quality of the ham, so find a butcher you can trust. If you do not wish to make a whole ham, buy a smaller 7- to 8-pound butt-end, bone in.

½ **cup Dijon-style mustard**
1 **cup firmly packed dark brown sugar**
1 **10-pound cooked ham, bone in, scored ½- to ¾-inch deep in a diamond pattern with scores ½ inch apart**
1 **quart apple cider or juice**

Preheat the oven to 350°. Rub the mustard over the ham to coat, then carefully pat on the brown sugar. Put the ham in a shallow roasting pan and pour in the apple cider. Bake for 1 to 1½ hours, basting frequently, until heated through and crusty. Slice the ham, transfer it to a large platter, and serve.

SERVES 12 OR MORE

The unsliced omelet garnished with watercress.

Sweet Potato Chips

A most pleasant and unexpected use of the sweet potato. Be sure to use fresh, clean oil.

> 6 **large sweet potatoes or yams, peeled**
> **Vegetable oil**
> **Salt**

With an adjustable-blade mandoline or by hand with a sharp knife, cut the potatoes into round slices as thin as possible.

Deep fry in small batches in vegetable oil that has been heated to 350°. Turn often and fry for 45 seconds to 1 minute, until golden. (Sweet potatoes will take a little longer to cook than yams.) The chips are done when the edges are slightly curled. Drain on paper towels and salt to taste. Serve immediately or at room temperature.

NOTE: The chips may be made 2 hours in advance. To reheat, preheat the oven to 425°. Spread the potatoes on a baking sheet and heat for 5 minutes.

VARIATION: To make potato straws, cut the potatoes either crosswise or lengthwise into sticks about ¼ inch × ¼ inch. Cook as above, turning often until golden.

SERVES 12

Layered Omelet

A colorful and pretty variation of the omelet that is easy to make for a crowd because the eggs are scrambled and baked.

> 1 **pound fresh spinach, trimmed, or**
> 1 **package frozen chopped spinach,**
> **defrosted, drained, and squeezed dry**
> 13 **tablespoons unsalted butter**
> **Freshly ground nutmeg, to taste**
> **Salt and freshly ground black pepper, to taste**
> 1 **cup finely chopped leeks (white part only)**
> ¼ **pound Brie, thoroughly chilled**
> 3 **medium tomatoes, peeled, seeded, and chopped**
> ½ **teaspoon dried thyme**
> 24 **eggs**
> 1 **teaspoon salt**
> ¼ **cup heavy cream**

> **GARNISH**
> **Sprigs of watercress**

In a covered pan, cook the spinach in the water clinging to the leaves just until wilted. Drain and squeeze dry. In a skillet, heat 3 tablespoons butter. Add the spinach, nutmeg, and salt and pepper and cook until the moisture has evaporated. Transfer to a bowl and set aside.

Wipe out the skillet, heat another 3 tablespoons butter, and sauté the leeks until softened. Season with salt and pepper, transfer to another bowl, and set aside. With a very sharp knife, scrape the rind from the Brie and thinly slice. Set aside.

Wipe out the skillet and heat 3 more tablespoons of butter. Over medium high heat, sauté the tomatoes, stirring occasionally, until the moisture has evaporated. Add the thyme and salt and pepper to taste. Transfer to another bowl and set aside.

Blackberries make these muffins special.

Preheat the oven to 375°. Heavily butter the bottom and sides of a loaf pan, 10½ × 5 × 2½ inches, line with buttered parchment paper or a reusable nonstick lining sheet (available at specialty cookware stores), and set aside.

In a large bowl, whisk the eggs with 1 teaspoon salt and pepper to taste. Set aside 1 cup of eggs, and divide the rest evenly between 2 bowls. Using 2 tablespoons butter and 1 bowl of eggs, make softly scrambled eggs in a large skillet. Transfer to a plate. Repeat with the remaining butter and second bowl of eggs. Combine the reserved 1 cup eggs with the cream. Pour two-thirds of this mixture into the prepared pan. Layer the scrambled eggs, a fourth at a time, with the spinach, leeks, Brie, and then tomatoes. The last layer should be scrambled eggs. Pour the remaining egg-cream mixture over the top, letting it seep down around the layers.

Cover the pan with buttered parchment paper or a reusable nonstick lining sheet. Put the loaf pan in a larger baking pan and add enough hot water to reach halfway up the sides of the loaf pan. Bake the omelet for 35 to 40 minutes, until it is set. Let sit for 5 minutes, then remove the parchment paper or lining sheet and invert onto a serving platter. Remove the remaining parchment paper or lining sheet. Let stand for about 10 minutes to facilitate slicing. Serve warm, garnished with watercress.

NOTE: The spinach, leek, and tomato mixtures may be prepared a day ahead and refrigerated. Do not make the eggs or assemble until just before baking.

SERVES 12

Blackberry Muffins

Blackberries provide a pleasant change from blueberries in these muffins. Note the use of margarine, which in this case results in a lighter muffin.

- **4 tablespoons (½ stick) margarine (not butter), at room temperature**
- **1 cup sugar**
- **1 cup milk**
- **1 egg, beaten**
- **1⅓ cups unbleached all-purpose flour**
- **2 teaspoons baking powder**
- **¾ teaspoon cinnamon**
- **¾ teaspoon nutmeg**
- **¼ teaspoon salt**
- **½ teaspoon vanilla extract**
- **1 cup fresh blackberries (or dry frozen)**

Preheat the oven to 375°. Grease 12 muffin tins heavily and set aside.

Cream the margarine and sugar in an electric mixer on low speed until light and fluffy. Add the milk, egg, ⅔ cup flour, baking powder, cinnamon, nutmeg, salt, and vanilla. Beat just until blended.

By hand, fold in the remaining ⅔ cup flour. The batter should still be lumpy. Fill muffin tins three quarters full and carefully place a few blackberries on top of each muffin. Bake for 20 to 30 minutes, until the muffins are golden brown. Let cool in the pans for 5 to 10 minutes. Remove and let cool on a rack. (These muffins are sticky, so loosen around the edges before turning out.) Serve warm.

MAKES 12 MUFFINS

BEVERLY HILLS

The strong Spanish-Mexican heritage of Los Angeles is evident in the red tile roofs and the street names reminding us of heroes and land grants, but in nothing more than its love of Mexican food—the somewhat different version developed by the Pueblo Indians.

Isolated along the Rio Grande and not much influenced by either the Spanish or the Aztecs in Mexico City, the Pueblos augmented the usual basics of Latin American countries—beans, squash, and corn—with game, berries, grasses, nuts, and chilies. These became the tacos, chiles rellenos, enchiladas, refried beans, etc., with which Los Angeles was well content until chefs began to experiment with reconciling the old ways with the new.

The fiesta was the grand gesture of the Mexican landowners. An entire village would be invited to a day of feasting. Food was prepared by the ton—whole steers barbecued in pits, huge pots of beans simmered on open fires, tortillas stacked until they toppled, salsas overflowing washtubs.... The somewhat smaller but no less lively fiesta arranged on the grounds of an old Spanish colonial home in Beverly Hills carried on the tradition. The spacious dignity of the house, with its sweep of lawn and majestic view, was an entirely appropriate background.

There were California innovations in the traditional dishes, and skewered steak on a grill instead of a steer in a pit—but the mariachis played as merrily as ever, and fiesta was the mood.

Chilies are important in these recipes, and some are hotter than others. Among the most common: ancho, round, very dark red when dried, mild but pungent; serrano, small, green, and mildly hot; pasilla, thin, long, mahogany-colored, mildly hot; negro or mulato, large, dark, very pungent; jalapeño, green and very hot. The degree of hotness can be modified in all of these recipes by varying the amount of chilies used.

MEXICAN FIESTA

FOR 16

Soft Tacos de Carnitas with Onions, Cilantro,
and Red Chili Salsa

Barbecued Mexican Gulf Shrimp

Barbecued Skewered New York Steak
Marinated in Adobo Spices

Clams on the Half Shell with Tomatillo Salsa

Deep-Fried Tripe with Mole Colorado

Barbecued Skewered Turkey Breast in
Mole Poblano and Sesame Seeds

Zucchini Blossom Quesadillas with Mexicana Salsa

Guacamole with Tortilla Chips

Chorizo Tostadas

Radishes • Jalapeño Chilies

Almond Tuiles • Coconut-Caramel Flan

Assorted Ices: Banana, Lime, Strawberry, and Papaya

Margaritas and Ice-Cold Beer

. . . .

Soft Tacos de Carnitas with Onions, Cilantro, and Red Chili Salsa

Soft tacos are easier to handle than the crisp. The ingredients also could be set forth—on hot plates as appropriate—with guests allowed to construct their own. The potent red chili salsa is best with the pork.

- 2 pounds pork butt, cut into ¼-pound pieces
- 16 corn tortillas

RED CHILI SALSA
MAKES ABOUT 1 CUP

- 30 Japanese chilies, stems removed (see Note)
- ½ white onion, coarsely chopped
- 5 medium garlic cloves
- 3 tomatoes, peeled, seeded, and coarsely chopped
- 1 teaspoon salt
- 1 onion, minced
- 2 bunches of cilantro, coarsely chopped

Simmer the pork pieces in water for 1½ to 2 hours, until tender. Drain. Preheat the oven to 450°. Roast the pork on a rack in a shallow pan for 1 hour or more. Coarsely chop and set aside.

Lower the oven to 300° and warm the tortillas, stacked in foil, for 20 minutes or more, until heated through.

Blend all the salsa ingredients together in a food processor fitted with the steel blade. Add a little water if necessary to make a saucelike consistency.

Put 2 to 3 tablespoons of pork on each tortilla and top with onion, cilantro, and a small amount of the salsa. Fold in half or roll up like a cigar.

NOTE: Care must be taken when handling chilies; the oils can burn eyes and skin. Wear gloves, and remove seeds and stems under running water.

SERVES 16 AS PART OF A BUFFET

Soft tacos de carnitas in a black Mexican bowl (far left). Crisp homemade tortilla chips sprinkled with salt and lime accompany margaritas (left).

Barbecued Mexican Gulf Shrimp

Annatto (variously spelled, and also called achiote) are the dried orange-red seeds from a tropical American tree. They add a delicate flavor, and a deep golden-orange color.

ANNATTO (ACHIOTE) OIL
MAKES 1 CUP

½ cup olive oil

½ cup lard, cut into pieces

2 1¼-ounce packages (about ½ cup) annatto (achiote) seeds

32 small garlic cloves, coarsely chopped

2 ancho chilies, stems and seeds removed, coarsely chopped (see Note, page 147)

Salt to taste

16 Mexican Gulf or other jumbo shrimp, peeled and deveined

To make annatto oil, over low heat melt the oil and lard in a saucepan. Add the annatto seeds and stir for 30 seconds. Raise the heat and bring the mixture to a boil. Simmer for 10 minutes. The mixture will turn red. Remove from the heat and let cool. Strain out the seeds. If not using immediately, cover tightly and refrigerate. (Annatto oil will keep for several months in the refrigerator, but its flavor will diminish with age.)

Sauté the garlic and ancho chilies in annatto oil until the garlic is soft but not browned. Add salt.

Prepare a barbecue. Run a water-soaked bamboo skewer lengthwise through the back of each shrimp, keeping it straight. Cook the shrimp on the barbecue for 3 minutes on each side, just until they turn opaque.

Arrange the shrimp on a platter and pour the oil, garlic, and chili mixture over them. Serve immediately.

SERVES 16 AS PART OF A BUFFET

Barbecued Skewered New York Steak Marinated in Adobo Spices

The true aficionado will probably be able to distinguish among the fiery subtleties of the three chilies, and everyone else will be interested according to their degree of tolerance.

ADOBO SPICE PASTE

1 pasilla chili, stems and seeds removed, coarsely chopped (see Note, page 147)

2 negro chilies, stems and seeds removed, coarsely chopped

2 ancho chilies, stems and seeds removed, coarsely chopped

2 tablespoons lard

1 small French-style roll, about 6 inches long, cut in half

1 tablespoon distilled vinegar

2 medium garlic cloves

1 tablespoon sugar

1 teaspoon salt

1 teaspoon oregano

2 cups (approximately) chicken stock, preferably homemade (page 17)

1½ pounds New York steak, preferably prime

GARNISH

1 bunch of cilantro, finely chopped
Lime wedges

To make the adobo spice paste, brown the chilies in the lard, remove with a slotted spoon, and set aside. Break the French roll into several pieces and fry in the lard until crisp and dry. Put the chilies, French roll, vinegar, garlic, sugar, salt, and oregano in a food processor fitted with the steel blade and process for 3 minutes, adding a little chicken stock, if necessary, to make a fine paste. Combine the paste and the remaining chicken stock in a saucepan and cook for 45 minutes, until the mixture thickens again into a fine paste. Set aside.

Trim the steak and cut it diagonally into ¼-inch-thick slices. Skewer, don't thread, the meat lengthwise on water-soaked bamboo skewers so that the wood does not show. Brush with the adobo spice paste and chill for at least 2 hours.

Prepare a barbecue. Grill the meat for 30 to 60 seconds per side. Watch carefully. Serve on a heated platter, sprinkled with cilantro and garnished with lime.

SERVES 16 AS PART OF A BUFFET

Clams on the Half Shell with Tomatillo Salsa

The lime juice will "cook" the clams. The milder tomatillo salsa is in order here, so as not to overwhelm the delicate little mollusks.

32 littleneck clams, rinsed and scrubbed

1½ cups freshly squeezed and strained lime juice

TOMATILLO SALSA
MAKES ABOUT 1½ CUPS

5 tomatillos (small green Mexican tomatoes), husks removed, and quartered

3 bunches of cilantro

5 medium garlic cloves

8 serrano chilies, stems and seeds removed (see Note, page 147)

1 teaspoon salt

Open the clams and remove them from their shells, reserving the shells. Try to keep the clams whole. Marinate in the lime juice for 5 to 10 minutes, no longer.

To make the salsa, blend all the ingredients in a food processor fitted with the steel blade. Add a little water if necessary to make a saucelike consistency.

Arrange the half shells on a platter. Put the clams back in the shells. Spoon the salsa on top.

SERVES 16 AS PART OF A BUFFET

Deep-Fried Tripe with Mole Colorado

Mole simply means sauce more complicated than salsa, and *colorado* is red. So this is tripe given zip and flavor—and nicely disguised—in a mildly hot red sauce.

1 pound honeycomb tripe

MOLE COLORADO
MAKES ABOUT 3 CUPS

8 ounces tomatoes

6 dried ancho chilies, seeds and stems removed (see Note, page 147)

1 onion, diced

2 garlic cloves

½ heaping cup dry bread crumbs

½ heaping cup yellow cornmeal

6 tablespoons unbleached all-purpose flour

2 eggs, lightly beaten

1 pound lard

Cut the tripe into 2-inch pieces, cover with water, and simmer for about 2 hours, until tender. Drain the tripe and dry it.

To make the mole sauce, blanch the tomatoes in a pot of boiling water for 10 to 15 seconds. Reserve 1 cup of the blanching liquid. Peel, seed, and dice the tomatoes into chunks.

Cover the ancho chilies with the reserved 1 cup liquid and let stand for 30 minutes. Drain the chilies and purée in a food processor fitted with the steel blade, along with the onion, garlic, and tomatoes. Add water as necessary to made a saucelike consistency.

Mix the bread crumbs and cornmeal. Dip the tripe into flour, then egg, and finally into the bread crumb–cornmeal mixture. In a large pot, deep fryer, or wok, heat the lard to 350° and deep fry the tripe until crisp. Drain on paper towels. Serve hot with Mole Colorado.

SERVES 16 AS PART OF A BUFFET

A glass Mexican platter holds a tempting display of clams on the half shell topped with salsa.

Barbecued Skewered Turkey Breast in Mole Poblano and Sesame Seeds

Mexican legend has a convent in panic because there was nothing to feed an unexpected archbishop. The nuns put everything they had, including chocolate, into a sauce for one old turkey. Angels helping, the noble prelate was delighted.

MOLE POBLANO SAUCE
MAKES 3 TO 3 1/2 CUPS

- 6 or 7 ancho chilies (3 ounces)
- 2 cups (or more) boiling chicken stock, preferably homemade (page 17)
- 3 ounces blanched almonds, finely ground
- ½ cup coarsely chopped onion
- 2 small tomatoes, peeled, seeded, and coarsely chopped
- ¼ cup lightly packed seedless raisins
- 1 tablespoon sesame seeds
- 1 corn tortilla, broken into small pieces
- 1 teaspoon finely chopped garlic
- ½ teaspoon ground cinnamon
- ½ teaspoon ground cloves
- ½ teaspoon ground coriander seeds
- ½ teaspoon aniseed
- 6 tablespoons lard
- 3 ounces Mexican chocolate, broken into small pieces
  Salt, to taste

- 1 pound fresh turkey breast

GARNISH

- 1 tablespoon sesame seeds

Put the ancho chilies in a flameproof bowl, pour in boiling chicken stock to cover, and let sit for 30 minutes. Drain the chilies, reserving 2 cups of the chicken stock. Remove the seeds, stems, and ribs from the chilies (see Note, page 147) and set aside.

Put the almonds, onion, tomatoes, raisins, sesame seeds, tortilla, garlic, spices, and 4 tablespoons lard in a food processor fitted with the steel blade. Add the chilies and 1 cup of the reserved chicken stock. Blend to a smooth purée.

In a heavy saucepan, melt the remaining 2 tablespoons lard. Pour in the mole sauce and simmer it, stirring constantly, for about 5 minutes. Add the remaining 1 cup chicken broth and the chocolate. Cook, uncovered, over low heat, stirring frequently, until the chocolate is melted. Add salt if necessary. Cover and set aside.

Prepare a barbecue. Cut the turkey breast with the grain into strips 4 inches long, 1 inch wide, and ⅛

inch thick. Place on water-soaked bamboo skewers lengthwise, being careful to skewer (not thread) the meat, so that the wood does not show through. Grill for 1 minute on each side. Place on a heated platter, cover with mole sauce, and sprinkle with sesame seeds.

SERVES 16 AS PART OF A BUFFET

. . . .

Zucchini Blossom Quesadillas with Mexicana Salsa

Zucchini blossoms have begun to brighten local markets—and lovely they are, with a delicate flavor. Mexicana salsa is a good, all-around salsa, fresh-tasting and chunky, but the milder tomatillo salsa would be equally good with these quesadillas.

- 32 zucchini blossoms, trimmed and cut into quarters
  Vegetable oil
  Salt and freshly ground pepper, to taste
- 16 corn tortillas
- 1 pound Mexican or Monterey Jack cheese, grated

MEXICANA SALSA
MAKES ABOUT 1 1/2 CUPS

- 4 ripe firm medium tomatoes, peeled, seeded, and chopped
- ½ white onion, finely diced
- 2 to 3 serrano chilies, stems and seeds removed, finely minced (see Note, page 147)
- 1 small bunch of cilantro, finely chopped
- ½ teaspoon salt

Cut 16 pieces of aluminum foil into squares a little larger than the diameter of the tortillas.

Sauté the zucchini blossoms in a little hot vegetable oil over medium high heat for a few seconds, add salt and pepper, and drain on paper towels. Heat the tortillas one at a time over an open flame until soft. Put 1 ounce of grated cheese and a few pieces of zucchini blossom on each tortilla and roll up tightly like a cigar. Reroll tightly in aluminum foil, folding over the ends.

Mix all the salsa ingredients in a bowl. Make as close to serving time as possible.

Preheat the oven to 350° and heat the quesadillas for 10 to 15 minutes, until they are hot and the cheese is melted. (They may be heated on a barbecue instead.) Serve immediately on a warm platter with the salsa.

SERVES 16 AS PART OF A BUFFET

Brilliant bougainvillea and a bright Guatemalan cloth add to the fiesta mood. Mexican pottery holds (clockwise from the right): zucchini blossom quesadillas, skewered turkey breast, deep-fried tripe with mole colorado for dipping.

Guacamole

The avocado is a native of Mexico, and it is the Mexican variety that is grown so successfully in California. This is a proper guacamole, with chunks.

- **4** medium avocados
- **½** white onion, finely minced
- **1** bunch cilantro, finely minced
  Freshly squeezed lime juice, to taste
  Salt, to taste
  Tabasco sauce, to taste (optional)

Peel the avocados, reserving the pits. Coarsely chop. Add the remaining ingredients and mix gently. Adjust seasonings if necessary. Put the avocado pits in the mixture to keep it from darkening, cover, and refrigerate. Remove just before serving. Serve with Tortilla Chips (recipe follows).

MAKES 3 CUPS

. . . .

Tortilla Chips

Much better than any you can buy. Their flavor is enhanced by lime juice.

- **24** corn tortillas
- **2** to 3 pounds lard
- **4** limes, cut in half
  Salt to taste

Cut each tortilla into 6 wedges. In a large pot, deep fryer, or wok, heat the lard to 350° and deep fry the tortilla wedges in batches until crisp. Drain on paper towels. Squeeze the lime juice over the chips and sprinkle with salt. Serve warm.

VARIATION: To make round tortilla chips, cut each corn tortilla into 4 rounds using a biscuit cutter or a knife and proceed as above.

SERVES 16 AS PART OF A BUFFET

Guacamole on cactus leaves.

Chorizo Tostadas

Tostadas are simply small tortillas (2 to 5 inches) fried until crisp. Chorizo is Mexican sausage. It can be bought in links, sometimes in cans, in Mexican markets and specialty stores.

CHORIZO
- **1** pound lean pork
- **½** pound pork fat
- **5** medium garlic cloves
- **⅓** cup paprika
- **2** tablespoons cayenne pepper
- **1** cup chopped cilantro
- **1** ounce tequila
- **1** teaspoon salt

REFRIED BLACK BEANS
- **1** pound black beans
- **½** medium onion
  Chicken stock to cover (approximately 8 to 10 cups), preferably homemade (page 17)
- **2** ounces lard
  Salt, to taste

- **32** 2-inch round tortilla chips, homemade (see Variation, page 152) or store-bought
- **¼** cup shredded green cabbage
- **½** pint Mexican cream or sour cream
- **¼** pound queso anejo (Mexican cheese) or Parmesan cheese, grated
- **1** small bunch of cilantro, chopped

Grind all the ingredients for the chorizo in a meat grinder, or use a food processor fitted with the steel blade, using an on-off motion until evenly combined. Let sit, covered, in the refrigerator for 48 hours.

Wash and drain the beans. Discard any discolored ones. Put the beans in a saucepan with the onion. Add chicken stock to cover and bring to a boil. Reduce the heat and simmer for 2 hours, adding stock as necessary, until the beans are soft and mushy. Do not drain. There should be about 1½ cups liquid left in the pot.

Heat the lard in a skillet and add the beans and the remaining cooking liquid. Cook for 15 to 20 minutes over medium high heat, stirring constantly and mashing the beans occasionally with a potato masher. When the liquid is almost absorbed, add the salt and set aside. Keep warm.

Sauté the chorizo over medium high heat, stirring constantly to break up chunks, for 7 to 8 minutes, until cooked through. Set aside and keep warm.

To assemble, preheat the oven to 350°. Spread the beans on the tortilla chips and top with chorizo, cabbage, Mexican or sour cream, cheese, and cilantro. Bake for 5 to 10 minutes, until warmed through.

SERVES 16 AS PART OF A BUFFET

Chorizo tostadas with lime wedges.

Almond Tuiles

A lovely, crisp, delicate cookie that keeps well stored in an airtight container.

14 ounces sliced almonds
2 cups less 2 tablespoons sugar
½ cup unbleached all-purpose flour
6 egg whites, unbeaten
6 tablespoons (¾ stick) unsalted butter, melted and cooled
Milk

Mix the almonds, sugar, and flour in a bowl. Blend in the egg whites and butter. Let rest for 1 hour.

Preheat the oven to 350° and prepare a baking sheet with oiled parchment paper. Dip a teaspoon into a small bowl of milk, take out a rounded spoonful of the cookie mixture, and put it on the parchment paper. With the back of the spoon, spread the batter into a round as thin as possible. Continue in this fashion, making sure to allow about 1½ inches between cookies. Bake for 12 to 14 minutes, until golden brown.

To shape the cookies into tuiles, while still warm, remove them from the baking sheet with a spatula one at a time and drape over a broom handle suspended between two chairs. While the first batch is cooling, form and bake the next batch. As the cookies cool they will become crisper.

MAKES ABOUT 48 COOKIES

Coconut-Caramel Flan

Flan, of Spanish origin, is the standard dessert of all Latin America. Coconut adds another taste.

CARAMEL
1 cup sugar
1½ tablespoons water
3 drops freshly squeezed lemon juice

7 ounces shredded unsweetened coconut

CUSTARD
4⅓ cups milk
1 vanilla bean, split in half lengthwise
4 eggs
8 egg yolks
1 cup sugar

To make the caramel, put the sugar, water, and lemon juice in a small saucepan. Over low heat, stir to dissolve the sugar. When the mixture comes to a boil, raise the heat to medium and, without stirring, let the sugar syrup cook for 8 to 10 minutes, until golden brown. Quickly pour the caramel into an ungreased 8-cup mold, swirling it so that the caramel covers the bottom and sides. Let cool.

Preheat the oven to 350°. Put the coconut on a baking sheet and toast, stirring often, for 10 to 12 minutes, until golden. Let cool.

Reduce the oven to 325°. To make the custard, bring the milk to a boil with the vanilla bean, and remove the vanilla bean. In a mixing bowl, beat the eggs, egg yolks, and sugar. Stirring constantly, add the hot milk to the egg mixture. Add the coconut. Pour into the caramelized mold, set the mold into a deep pan slightly larger than the mold, and fill the pan with boiling water to come halfway up the sides of the mold. Bake for approximately 1 hour. To be certain the custard is done, insert a knife blade into the center. It should come out clean. Remove from the oven and let cool. Run a knife between the custard and the outside of the mold. Turn out onto a platter deep enough to hold the liquid caramel that will run down the sides of the custard. Let cool slightly before serving.

SERVES 16 AS PART OF A BUFFET

A choice of desserts includes fresh fruit ices, coconut-caramel flan, and almond tuiles.

These ices are simple to make, and a lovely presentation with all the fresh fruit colors. Welcome, too, after the many chilies.

. . . .

Basic Sugar Syrup

This sugar syrup is the base for all the ices that follow. It keeps for several months.

4¼ **cups water**
5 **cups granulated sugar**

Put the water and sugar in a large saucepan. Place over medium heat and stir with a wooden spoon until the sugar has dissolved. When the syrup comes to a full boil, immediately remove the saucepan from the heat, let cool completely, and pour the syrup into a large jar. Cover and refrigerate.

MAKES 6⅓ CUPS

. . . .

Banana Ice

1¾ **pounds (4 to 6) ripe bananas**
1⅓ **cups cold Sugar Syrup (above)**
 Juice of ½ lime, strained
 ¾ **cup nonsparkling mineral water**
 2 **teaspoons rum (preferably white)**

Peel the bananas and process to a smooth purée in a food processor fitted with the steel blade. You will need 1⅔ cups of purée.

In a large bowl, mix the purée with the sugar syrup, lime juice, mineral water, and rum. Freeze in an ice-cream freezer according to the manufacturer's instructions (or see Note below). Transfer to a plastic container and keep frozen until serving time.

MAKES ABOUT 1 QUART

. . . .

Lime Ice

6½ **tablespoons freshly squeezed and strained lime juice**
6½ **tablespoons freshly squeezed and strained lemon juice**
1⅓ **cups nonsparkling mineral water**
1⅔ **cups cold Sugar Syrup (above)**
 1 **egg white**

Combine the lime and lemon juices and pour into an ice-cream freezer. Add the mineral water and sugar syrup and freeze according to the manufacturer's instruc-

tions (or see Note below). About 10 minutes before the ice is finished, stop the machine and remove 2 tablespoons of the mixture. Whisk vigorously with the egg white until thick and foamy. Pour into the ice-cream freezer and finish freezing. Transfer to a plastic container and keep frozen until serving time.

MAKES ABOUT 1 QUART

. . . .

Strawberry Ice

2½ **pints fresh strawberries**
 2 **cups cold Sugar Syrup (opposite)**
 1 **tablespoon freshly squeezed and strained lime juice (optional)**

Rapidly rinse the strawberries under cold running water, and stem them. Using a food processor fitted with the steel blade, process the berries to a smooth purée. You will need 2⅓ cups purée. If desired, lime juice may be added to heighten the taste.

In a large bowl, mix the purée with the sugar syrup. Freeze in an ice-cream freezer according to the manufacturer's instructions (or see Note below). Transfer to a plastic container and keep frozen until serving time.

MAKES ABOUT 3 CUPS

. . . .

Papaya Ice

1¾ **pounds (2 large) ripe papayas**
1⅓ **cups cold Sugar Syrup (opposite)**
 Juice of 1 lime, strained

With a paring knife, peel the papayas and discard the seeds. Place the papaya pulp in a food processor fitted with the steel blade and process to a smooth purée. You will need 2 cups of purée.

Place the purée in a large bowl and stir in the sugar syrup and lime juice. Freeze the mixture in an ice-cream freezer according to the manufacturer's instructions (or see Note below). Transfer to a plastic container and keep frozen until serving time.

MAKES ABOUT 3 CUPS

NOTE: If you do not have an ice-cream freezer, simply place the mixture in shallow metal pans and freeze until firm. Transfer to a food processor and process until smooth and fluffy. Serve immediately, or return to the freezer until serving time. For the best flavor, ices should be served within 2 or 3 days.

San Francisco

No dashing through the snow to grandmother's house for this holiday dinner. The hostess lives in a penthouse with all of San Francisco and both bridges at her feet. Her guests were not seated at a table presided over by a turkey with a formidable entourage of accompaniments and five different pies waiting in the kitchen. If California cooking has anything to teach, it is that we can have our cake and not eat it, too. All those traditional holiday tastes need only be rearranged—and glamorized.

Wild rice in the goose not only took the place of bread stuffing, mashed potatoes, and candied yams, it did so with grace. Onions in a soufflé were better and more dramatic than creamed, and who could pine for more vegetables—and a salad—when broccoli was served fresh and green in a lively vinaigrette? Cranberries made their appearance last, as a natural tartness in a properly rich chocolate torte.

That this was a special occasion, a warm, gracious, and sentimental day, was indicated not only by the care and thought in preparing the meal, but by the splendor of its setting. It happened to be an apartment particularly suited to California cooking, in that it combines the best of the old with the best of the new. Fine old tapestries and antique furniture are perfectly at ease with the mirrors, the marble, and the tall green growing things of modern living.

There were candles on the table, and red and white tulips. No heaviness settled over guests facing the obligation to eat too much. They talked easily and wittily. They rose to toast the hostess for her wisdom and her cooking skill. They were happy, and there was laughter.

HOLIDAY DINNER

FOR **8**

Celery Root Bisque

Roast Goose with Apricot Wild Rice Stuffing

Broccoli with Parsley Vinaigrette

Creamy Onion Soufflé

Cranberry-Chocolate Torte with Frosted Cranberries

WINES:

Dry Sherry with Bisque

Cabernet Sauvignon with Goose

Sparkling Muscat with Dessert

Celery Root Bisque

Celery root is not a taste beloved by everyone, but it has been subdued in this bisque to a mysterious subtlety. It can be made two or three days ahead, gently reheated, or even served cold.

- 4 cups celery root (about 1½ pounds), peeled and cubed
- ¼ cup chopped scallions
- 5 tablespoons unsalted butter
- 6 cups chicken stock, preferably homemade (page 17)
- 2 cups peeled and cubed potatoes
- 1 large parsnip, peeled and chopped
  Salt and freshly ground black pepper, to taste
- 2 egg yolks, beaten
- ½ cup heavy cream

GARNISH
  Fresh chervil
  Celery slices, cut on the diagonal

Sauté the celery root and scallions in the butter over moderately high heat for 5 minutes. Add the chicken stock, potatoes, parsnip, and salt and pepper. Bring to a boil. Cook, covered, over moderate heat for 25 minutes, until the vegetables are tender. Remove from the heat and strain, reserving the liquid.

In a food processor fitted with the steel blade, purée the solids with ½ cup of the liquid until smooth. Combine with the rest of the liquid.

In a small bowl, whisk the egg yolks into the cream. Add ½ cup of the soup in a stream, stirring, and then return this mixture to the soup.

Heat the soup, stirring, but do not let it boil. Correct seasonings and serve immediately, garnished with fresh chervil and celery slices.

SERVES 8

The celery root bisque is garnished with celery and chervil (far left). Generous portions of the holiday goose are served with all the trimmings (left).

Roast Goose with Apricot– Wild Rice Stuffing

The problem with goose has always been the fat, but poaching it, as New York cooking teacher Lydie Marshall recommends, helps with that. Apricots lighten the stuffing and balance the richness of the goose.

- 1 **12-pound goose**
  Salt and freshly ground black pepper, to taste

APRICOT–WILD RICE STUFFING
MAKES 9 TO 10 CUPS

- 3 **cups dried apricots, soaked overnight in equal amounts of dry sherry and water, to cover**
- ½ **cup minced fresh parsley**
- ½ **teaspoon ground mace**
- ½ **teaspoon freshly grated nutmeg**
- ½ **teaspoon ground cloves**
- 1 **teaspoon dried thyme**
- 1 **cup pine nuts, toasted**
- 8 **cups cooked wild rice (see Note)**
- 1 **cup (2 sticks) unsalted butter**
- 1 **cup chopped scallions**
- 1½ **cups minced celery leaves**
  Salt and freshly ground black pepper, to taste

- 1 **slice of bread**
- 1 **teaspoon salt**
- 8 **tablespoons (1 stick) unsalted butter**
- ½ **cup water**
  Salt and freshly ground black pepper, to taste

Before roasting, poach the goose to make it more tender. Salt and pepper the cavity of the goose and put it in a large roasting pan. Cover with boiling water and add 2 tablespoons salt. Bring the water back to a boil and simmer for about 1 hour. Drain the goose well. Remove all fat from the top of the poaching liquid, reserving 2 to 3 tablespoons, and discard the poaching liquid. (Refrigerate or freeze the rest of the goose fat in a tightly sealed plastic container. It is excellent for sautéeing potatoes and other vegetables.)

While the goose is being poached, make the stuffing. Drain and chop the apricots. Put them in a large bowl and add the parsley, mace, nutmeg, cloves, thyme, pine nuts, and wild rice. Melt the butter in a large skillet. Pour all but 2 to 3 tablespoons butter over the wild rice mixture and stir to combine. In the remaining butter, sauté the scallions and celery leaves. Add to the wild rice mixture, mix well, and add salt and pepper to taste.

Preheat the oven to 350°. Fill the goose loosely with the stuffing and seal with the slice of bread. Leftover stuffing may be heated separately (as may all of the stuffing if you choose not to stuff the goose) in a covered dish in a 350° oven.

Truss the goose and place it, breast side up, in a greased roasting pan. Add the reserved goose fat to the pan. Rub the breast of the goose with 4 to 5 tablespoons butter and sprinkle with about 1 teaspoon salt. Roast on the middle rack in the oven, pricking the skin occasionally so that the fat will run out. Remove the rendered fat as the goose roasts, leaving ¼ cup in the pan to occasionally baste the goose. The goose will be done in 1½ to 2 hours, when the skin is dark brown and it crackles under the teeth.

Transfer the goose to a cutting board with a juice catcher. Reserving the pan juices, remove the stuffing and carve the goose.

Remove all the fat possible from the juices in the roasting pan and any burned particles at the bottom of the pan. Reheat the remaining drippings with the reserved juices from the cutting board and ½ cup water, scraping the sides and bottom of the pan to incorporate the drippings. Boil for 1 minute, remove the pan from the flame, and whisk in the remaining 3 tablespoons butter, a tablespoon at a time. Season with salt and pepper and serve the sauce with the goose.

NOTE: Cook the wild rice the night before and refrigerate until ready to use so that it will be well dried. For 8 cups cooked wild rice, use 2¾ cups uncooked rice and follow the instructions on the package.

SERVES 8

Fresh broccoli, cooked to perfection, needs nothing more than a light dressing.

Broccoli with Parsley Vinaigrette

Broccoli is of the cabbage family and related to cauliflower, but is greener, prettier, and fresher-tasting than its relatives. The vinaigrette dressing with parsley and chives is also smartly green and fresh.

2½ to 3 pounds broccoli, well trimmed, cut into flowerettes with 1 to 2 inches of stem
  6 tablespoons white wine vinegar
1½ teaspoons Dijon-style mustard
  ¾ cup vegetable oil
  ½ cup snipped fresh chives
  ¾ cup fresh minced parsley
  3 tablespoons finely minced shallots
  1 teaspoon salt
    Freshly ground black pepper, to taste

Drop the broccoli into boiling salted water and cook for 8 to 10 minutes, until the stems are easily pierced with a fork. Drain well.

While the broccoli is cooking, combine the vinegar and mustard in a small bowl. Slowly whisk in the oil, and continue whisking until the vinaigrette is emulsified. Add the chives, parsley, shallots, salt, and pepper and mix well. Pour enough dressing over the hot, well-drained broccoli to coat. Serve warm or let cool to room temperature.

S E R V E S 8

. . . .

Creamy Onion Soufflé

A soufflé always brings an aura of the special—and does it not make an aristocrat of the homely onion?

  6 tablespoons (¾ stick) unsalted butter
  3 medium onions, peeled and finely chopped (about 4 cups)
  3 tablespoons unbleached all-purpose flour
1½ cups heavy cream
  ½ teaspoon sage
    Salt and freshly ground white pepper, to taste
10 egg whites, at room temperature

GARNISH
    Thin slices of onion sautéed in a small amount of butter

Butter a 2-quart soufflé dish and set aside.

Melt 3 tablespoons butter in a heavy skillet and sauté the onions, stirring occasionally until the moisture has evaporated; *do not* let the onions become so dry that they stick to the pan. Set aside and let cool.

Melt the remaining 3 tablespoons butter in a saucepan and add the flour, whisking rapidly. Cook for 2 to 3 minutes, but do not let it brown. Remove the pan from the heat and whisk in the cream vigorously. Return the pan to the stove and continue to whisk over low heat until the mixture is very thick. Remove from the heat and add the sage and salt and pepper. When the mixture has cooled, add the cooked onions.

Preheat the oven to 375°. Beat the egg whites until they form soft peaks. Stir a quarter of the egg whites into the onion mixture. Gently fold in the remaining whites, a third at a time.

Spoon the mixture into the prepared dish and bake for 35 minutes, until puffed, set, and brown. If desired, garnish with sautéed onion slices. Serve immediately.

N O T E : This soufflé may be prepared ahead up to the point where the egg whites are whipped and folded in.

S E R V E S 8

The grand pouf of the onion soufflé is a dramatic compliment to the guests.

Chocolate-Cranberry Torte with Frosted Cranberries

Cranberries honor that first thankful dinner, when they undoubtedly appeared in a sauce with honey or maple syrup, as the Indians had taught the Pilgrims. Tradition is well served by adding their tartness to this dense, rich chocolate dessert.

- 1 **16-ounce can of whole-berry cranberry sauce**
- ½ **cup ground blanched almonds**
- ¼ **cup sifted unbleached all-purpose flour**
- 7 **ounces semisweet chocolate, coarsely chopped**
- 8 **tablespoons (1 stick) unsalted butter**
- 3 **eggs, separated**
- ½ **cup sugar**
- ¼ **teaspoon almond extract**
- **Pinch of salt**

CHOCOLATE GLAZE

- 6 **ounces semisweet chocolate, coarsely chopped**
- ¾ **cup heavy cream**
- 1 **to 1½ tablespoons water (optional)**

FROSTED CRANBERRY GARNISH

- **Fresh cranberries, washed and well dried**
- 1 **egg white**
- **Superfine sugar**

- **Green marzipan leaves or fresh mint (optional)**

Put a rack in the bottom third of the oven and preheat the oven to 350°. Grease and flour a 9-inch springform pan.

Put the cranberry sauce in a small bowl and gently stir until slightly liquid. In another small bowl, combine the ground almonds and flour. Set both bowls aside.

In a double boiler, over hot water, melt the chocolate and butter, stirring occasionally to blend. Remove from the heat and set aside.

In a large bowl, beat the egg yolks and sugar until thick and light. With the mixer on low, add the almond-flour mixture, beating just until combined. Gently fold in the chocolate-butter mixture. Stir in the reserved cranberry sauce and the almond extract.

In a medium bowl, with clean dry beaters, beat the egg whites with a pinch of salt until they hold their shape but are not dry. Gently fold the whites into the batter. Pour the batter into the prepared pan, using a rubber spatula to smooth the surface gently. Bake for 55 minutes. The torte will still look soupy in the middle but

will solidify as it cools. Let cool completely in the pan, and put in the refrigerator for at least an hour, until chilled. Release the torte from the pan and invert it onto a rack. The top of the torte will now be the bottom.

To make the chocolate glaze, melt the chocolate with the cream in a small heavy saucepan. Stir often and bring just to a boil. Let cool to lukewarm and add water, if necessary, to make a runny consistency.

Place wax paper under the rack and quickly pour all of the glaze over the torte. Tilt to get the glaze to cover the top, then all of the sides, using a long metal spatula to aid you. Lift the wire rack and tap gently to smooth the sides and let excess chocolate run off. When the glaze has cooled, transfer the torte to a serving plate.

To prepare the frosted cranberry garnish, dip each cranberry in the unbeaten egg white, then in superfine sugar. Place on wax paper and let the berries sit at room temperature until dried. Do not refrigerate.

Just before serving, decorate the top of the torte with frosted cranberries, and additional fresh cranberries and marzipan leaves or fresh mint, if desired.

MAKES ONE 9-INCH TORTE

The chocolate-cranberry torte is decorated for the holidays with marzipan leaves, and frosted and unfrosted cranberries.

RUSSIAN HILL

The stranger in San Francisco—riding the cable cars, strolling the museums, finding the Bay at the end of almost every street—immediately falls in love. San Francisco is an enchanted city, soaring on its hills, the Bay spread around it like a silken skirt.

San Franciscans take pride in everything—the Embarcadero freeway they stopped halfway to nowhere, the cable cars they saved, the memory of Gold Rush bravado.... They love their restaurants and the artist-haunted cafés, the Opera, the Golden Gate Bridge, the rain, the Civic Center, Telegraph Hill.... It is a satisfied city.

This art dealer's charming two-story house on Russian Hill overlooks a tiny courtyard and the Bay beyond, and boasts a cable car just outside the door. The house is filled with art, a joyful, whimsical, priceless, wide-ranging collection that allows Mickey and Minnie Mouse to guard the fireplace while three Picasso vases stand on the table with ceramic salt and pepper shakers made to look like tubes of paint.

The dinner was planned to be equally wide-ranging. It began with an almost Italian version of Japanese sashimi, followed by veal chops with wild mushrooms that find their origin in classical French cuisine. Thyme was the California touch distinguishing the potato galettes. Zucchini is a native of Italy, of course, but there is no evidence that Italians ever grated and sautéed it with lettuce, spinach, and greens; that would seem to be purely Californian. Boule de neige borrows a French name, but goes its own contemporary way as a rich chocolate mousse.

ECLECTIC DINNER

FOR 6

Sea Bass Sashimi

Veal Chops with Wild Mushrooms

Potato Galettes

Sauté of Zucchini and Mixed Greens

Boule de Neige

WINES:

Johannesberg Riesling with Sashimi

Full-Bodied Chardonnay or Pinot Noir with Veal

. . . .

Sea Bass Sashimi

There is more than a little Italian in this version of sashimi, which could be called sea bass carpaccio with equal validity. But to adapt and combine is, of course, a California characteristic. Take care that the sauce does not overwhelm the delicate fish. Whitefish or yellow fish could be substituted.

1½   **pounds very fresh sea bass**
       Salt and freshly ground white pepper, to taste
  2   **tablespoons freshly squeezed and strained lemon juice**
  2   **teaspoons tarragon or Dijon-style mustard**
10   **tablespoons oil, half vegetable and half extra virgin olive**
  1   **teaspoon finely chopped fresh tarragon**
  4   **Italian plum tomatoes, peeled, seeded, and finely chopped**
       Additional fresh tarragon and lemon juice (optional)
  1   **cup finely julienned daikon radish**

Have the fishmonger bone the fish and slice it very thinly on the diagonal. The slices should be about ¹⁄₁₆ inch thick. If they are not, place them between two pieces of plastic wrap and pound as thin as possible, being careful not to tear the fish.

Lightly salt and pepper one side of the sea bass slices. Arrange, seasoned side down, on individual serving plates. Cover and refrigerate.

In a small mixing bowl, mix the lemon juice and mustard. Slowly whisk in the oil and salt and pepper to taste. Stir in the tarragon.

Just before serving, spoon some of the dressing over the fish and turn the slices to moisten both sides. Scatter the tomato over the fish and sprinkle with additional fresh tarragon and lemon juice, if desired. Arrange a small amount of daikon radish on the side of each plate. Refrigerate, covered, for 15 minutes before serving.

SERVES 6 AS A FIRST COURSE

The sea bass sashimi is translucent on celadon plates. The paint tubes are really salt and pepper shakers, part of a whimsical collection of the owner.

Veal chops with wild mushroom sauce, potato galettes, and zucchini and greens sauté. Lilies are arranged in a Picasso pitcher; the painting in the background is by Richard Diebenkorn.

Veal Chops with Wild Mushrooms

Mushrooms—grandly imported, sometimes triumphantly discovered in our own mountains and back yards, and always eaten reverently—have become one of the symbols of California cooking.

- **4 tablespoons (½ stick) unsalted butter**
- **2 shallots, finely chopped**
- **1½ cups heavy cream**
- **½ cup Veal Stock (recipe follows)**
- **9 ounces wild mushrooms, rinsed briefly, dried, and trimmed: 3 ounces each oyster, shiitake, and black chanterelle mushrooms (see Note)**
- **6 loin veal chops, about 1 inch thick**
- **3 tablespoons olive oil**
  Salt and freshly ground black pepper, to taste

GARNISH
Fresh herbs or sprigs of watercress

Heat 2 tablespoons butter in a sauté pan, add the shallots, and sauté until softened. Add the cream and cook until thickened and reduced to approximately 1 cup. In a small saucepan, bring the veal stock to a boil and cook until syrupy and reduced to a glaze. Add to the cream mixture and set aside.

Slice or cut the mushrooms into smaller pieces, if desired. Melt the remaining 2 tablespoons butter in a skillet and quickly sauté the mushrooms over high heat until golden brown. Set aside and keep warm.

Rub the veal chops generously with olive oil, and season with salt and pepper. Heat a large cast iron skillet over high heat until it smokes. Sear the chops for 3 minutes on each side, remove from the pan, and keep warm. To deglaze the pan, pour off the excess fat and add the reserved cream mixture. Heat and stir, scraping any bits from the bottom and incorporating them into the sauce. Add the mushrooms and adjust the seasonings. Place the veal chops on individual plates and spoon some of the sauce over each chop. Garnish with fresh herbs or watercress.

NOTE: If the fresh mushrooms called for are not available, substitute any of the dried ones (cepes, porcini, chanterelles, morels). Rinse them well to get rid of any sand and reconstitute by soaking in warm water or Madeira for 30 minutes or more.

SERVES 6

Veal Stock

Another stock to keep ready in the freezer. It can be reduced as much as wished for convenience, even all the way down to a jelly.

- **10 pounds veal bones, or a combination of veal and chicken bones**
- **2 cups white wine, port, or Madeira**
- **2 carrots, scrubbed and cut into 1-inch pieces**
- **2 onions, peeled and cut in half**
- **1 celery stalk with leaves, cut into 1-inch pieces**
- **2 leeks (white part only), cleaned and cut into 1-inch pieces**
- **2 tomatoes, quartered**
- **1 large bay leaf**
- **10 peppercorns**
- **1½ teaspoons dried thyme**
- **2 sprigs of parsley**

Preheat the oven to 425°. Put the bones in a large roasting pan and bake, turning occasionally, for 1 hour, until well browned. Remove the bones to a large stockpot. Discard the excess grease from the roasting pan and deglaze on top of the stove with the wine, scraping up the brown bits on the bottom of the pan. Add this liquid to the stockpot, along with the vegetables and herbs. Pour in enough water to cover the bones and vegetables by 2 inches and bring to a boil. Turn down the heat and simmer slowly, partially covered, for 6 to 8 hours, skimming off the foam as it accumulates and adding water as necessary to keep the bones and vegetables covered.

When cool enough to handle, remove the bones and pour the stock through a fine-mesh strainer into a large bowl. Let cool to room temperature. Refrigerate until the fat rises to the top. Remove the fat and discard. The stock should be clear. Refrigerate for up to 3 days, or freeze in small covered containers.

MAKES ABOUT 4 QUARTS

Potato Galettes

Fresh herbs are easy to grow in the garden or on a sunny windowsill, and they are becoming available in supermarkets all over the country. Thyme makes this dish special.

   4 large baking potatoes (about 3 pounds)
   ¾ cup (1½ sticks) unsalted butter, melted
   1 tablespoon fresh thyme or 1 teaspoon dried
   1½ teaspoons salt
      Freshly ground black pepper, to taste

Preheat the oven to 450°. Set out six 4-inch round non-stick pans or one 12-inch nonstick frying pan with a heatproof handle.

Peel the potatoes and slice as thin as possible, preferably with a mandoline. As each potato is sliced, toss with some of the melted butter, making sure to coat each slice. Place a layer of potatoes on the bottom of each pan, overlapping the slices. Sprinkle with half the thyme and salt and pepper. Repeat with another layer, and dribble any remaining butter on top.

Bake for 30 to 45 minutes, until the surface is golden brown and crisp and the potatoes can easily be pierced with a fork. If using a 12-inch pan, cut into wedges to serve.

SERVES 6

. . . .

Sauté of Zucchini and Mixed Greens

This is a welcome fresh green on the plate, a counterpoint to the neutral colors, as well as the richness, of potatoes and veal.

   2 pounds zucchini, washed and trimmed
   1 teaspoon salt
   1 small head of Boston lettuce
   2 bunches of spinach, stems removed
   1 bunch of beet greens, stems removed
   2 bunches of dandelion greens, stems removed
   4 tablespoons (½ stick) unsalted butter
   2 tablespoons olive oil
   ½ cup minced onion
   2 medium garlic cloves, minced
      Salt and freshly ground black pepper, to taste

Using a grater, mandoline, or food processor, coarsely shred the zucchini. Sprinkle with salt and let stand for 20 minutes. Transfer to a colander, rinse well, and squeeze dry in a dish towel. Set aside.

Separately steam until tender the lettuce, spinach, beet greens, and dandelion greens. Squeeze dry in a clean dish towel. Coarsely chop and set aside.

Heat the butter and oil in a large sauté pan. Add the onion and garlic and sauté for 5 minutes. Add the zucchini and stir over medium high heat for 5 minutes more, until crisp-tender. Add the reserved greens and heat to warm through. Season with salt and pepper and serve immediately.

SERVES 6

. . . .

Boule de Neige

An elegant, dramatic dessert. If the rosettes seem daunting, the whipped cream can be applied with a spatula in a decorative fashion.

   12 ounces bittersweet or semisweet chocolate,
      cut into small pieces
   ¾ cup freshly brewed strong coffee
   1 cup sugar
   1½ cups (3 sticks) unsalted butter, at room temperature
   6 eggs, beaten

   1 cup heavy cream, whipped and sweetened to taste

GARNISH
      Peel of 1 orange, cut in a single ¼-inch-wide
      strip to form a spiral

Preheat the oven to 300°. Line a 1½- or 2-quart stainless steel or other ovenproof bowl with a single piece of heavy-duty foil. Make sure there are no tears in the foil.

Melt the chocolate with the coffee and sugar in a medium saucepan. Stir over moderate heat until the sugar is dissolved. Add the butter in pieces, whisking continually. Remove from the heat and quickly whisk in the eggs. Immediately strain the mixture into the foil-lined bowl. Place in the lower third of the oven and bake for 60 to 65 minutes, until it rises, cracks, and is crusty and dry around the edges. Let cool to room temperature, cover, and refrigerate overnight. The dessert will firm up as it chills.

To serve, invert the boule de neige onto a plate, peel off the foil, and trim the edges to make a nice dome shape. Using a pastry bag fitted with a star tip, pipe rosettes of sweetened whipped cream over the entire surface. Garnish with an orange peel spiral, if desired.

SERVES 6 OR MORE

Champagne flutes stand guard over the boule de neige, while Mickey and Minnie Mouse are on duty in front of the fireplace.

SAN FRANCISCO

Victorian homes were built to last, and nowhere have they lasted better than in San Francisco, where they are treasures to be dearly bought and carefully restored. They suggest a more leisured time, when ladies were "at home" on Thursdays, with news, gossip, and all sorts of social points to be gathered over a cup of tea poured from a silver pot. Today's ladies are more apt to be in their offices on Thursdays. Nevertheless, afternoon tea is being served—and welcomed—not only in old Victorian homes, but in smart new hotels and restaurants. Both ladies and gentlemen arrive with briefcases and news of the city. It is a civilized substitute for the cocktail party, suited to the moderation of today.

Learning about tea is as delightfully complicated as anything else—which is probably part of its present-day appeal. One must know the merchant who carries varietal teas in bulk, perhaps even distinguishing among the three harvests, or flushes. The classics would include Darjeeling, with its smooth muscatel flavor; the malty Assam; the delicate Keemuns and stronger Yunnans from China; and the great, sweetly smooth Oolongs of Taiwan.

An ample afternoon tea was set forth in this fine old Victorian home, restored to a contemporary interpretation of its former grandeur. The luxury of high ceilings, pillared walls, and fine fabrics remains, but lightened to only suggest the plush and flourish of the period. Its dignity dominates the sleek high-rises of Russian Hill.

The hostess will probably want to choose from among the following recipes—unless she has a fine old Victorian staff in the kitchen. The tea table does not require great variety, only a carefully selected array of favorite sandwiches, desserts, and, of course, tea.

AFTERNOON TEA

FOR **12** OR MORE

Tea Sandwiches

Smoked Trout Mousse on Toast Points

Currant Scones with Lemon-Maple Marmalade
and Rhubarb Conserve

Frangipani Tartlets

Chocolate-Mocha Torte

Chocolate-Dipped Shortbread Cookies

Citrus Pecans

Caraway Cake

Fresh Cherries

Assorted Teas

California Dry Sherry or Sweet Semillon

. . . .

Tea Sandwiches

These may be as various as you like. Consider the general effect. It is as important for tea sandwiches to look pretty as to taste good.

Make your own, or order ahead from a good bakery, a combination of breads such as white, wheat, limpa, and rye, and make sure they are sliced very thin. Remove the crusts from 8 to 10 slices of one kind of bread and stack the slices. Press together with a rolling pin until flattened. Peel the slices apart and, using a cookie cutter, biscuit cutter, or a sharp knife, cut into shapes such as fingers, rounds, and triangles; leave some slices whole to roll up. Spread each with softened unsalted butter or mayonnaise. Fill as desired and arrange on a large platter. Cover with a damp towel to keep the sandwiches from drying out.

SUGGESTED SANDWICHES:

Paper-thin slices of smoked turkey with homemade Mayonnaise (page 176) on rye bread

Steamed asparagus rolled in white bread with Lemon Mayonnaise (see Variation, page 176)

Sliced tomato and grated Gruyère cheese on buttered white bread

Deviled egg and watercress with homemade Mayonnaise (page 176) on wheat bread

Cream cheese, chutney, and finely chopped cashews on buttered wheat bread

Smoked salmon and dill sauce on Limpa Bread (page 176)

Mascarpone cheese on Black Bread (page 209)

Tea sandwiches are arranged on Victorian-style plates and cake stands, and an old silver biscuit jar holds roses and baby's breath (far left). An assortment of dainty sandwiches and pretty cakes to choose from makes tea-time a pleasant pause in the day's routine.

Mayonnaise

Simple to make with a food processor, mayonnaise lends itself to many delicious variations with the oils, vinegars, and herbs now available.

- **1 large egg, at room temperature**
- **2 teaspoons freshly squeezed and strained lemon juice**
- **1 teaspoon dry mustard**
- **Salt and freshly ground white pepper, to taste**
- **1½ cups vegetable oil**

Put the egg, lemon juice, mustard, salt, pepper, and 3 tablespoons vegetable oil in the bowl of a food processor fitted with the steel blade. Process until well mixed. With the machine running, slowly drizzle in the remaining oil in a steady stream. As the oil is added, the mayonnaise will thicken. Adjust the seasonings. Refrigerate in a covered jar for a week to 10 days.

VARIATION: To make lemon mayonnaise, increase the lemon juice to 1 tablespoon, add the grated rind of 1 lemon, and proceed as above.

MAKES 1¾ CUPS

. . . .

Limpa Bread

Scandinavians hold their bread in great respect, with at least three varieties stacked in a basket at every meal. They grow grains that can withstand the weather—mostly rye. Limpa can also be baked in round loaves on a cookie sheet.

- **1 package active dry yeast**
- **1 teaspoon sugar**
- **1 cup lukewarm water (105° to 115°)**
- **1 cup lukewarm milk (105° to 115°)**
- **4 cups unbleached all-purpose flour**
- **¾ cup dark corn syrup**
- **5⅓ tablespoons (⅓ cup) unsalted butter**
- **Grated rind of 1 orange (optional)**
- **1 teaspoon lightly crushed aniseed**
- **1 teaspoon lightly crushed fennel seed**
- **1½ teaspoons salt**
- **3 cups rye flour**
- **Yellow cornmeal**

Dissolve the yeast and sugar in the lukewarm water. Put the yeast mixture, lukewarm milk, and 3 cups all-purpose flour in a large mixing bowl and beat well. Cover with a damp towel and let rise in a warm place for 1¼ hours, until doubled.

In heavy saucepan combine the corn syrup, butter, orange rind (if used), aniseed, fennel seed, and salt. Slowly bring to a boil, then let cool. Beat into the dough. Add the rye flour and the remaining cup all-purpose flour to make a firm dough. Knead on a floured board for 8 to 10 minutes, until smooth and elastic. Put the dough in an oiled bowl and turn to coat well. Cover with a damp towel and let rise in a warm place for 1½ hours, until doubled.

Punch down and knead again for 3 to 4 minutes, until elastic. Divide the dough into 4 pieces and shape into loaves. Oil 4 bread pans, approximately 7½ × 3¾ × 2½ inches, and sprinkle cornmeal on the bottoms. Put the loaves in the pans, cover with a damp towel, and let rise again for 45 minutes, until doubled.

Preheat the oven to 375°. Bake for 25 to 30 minutes, until golden brown. Brush the tops with lukewarm water and bake for 5 minutes longer, until well browned. Remove the bread from the pans at once by loosening the sides with a metal spatula. Let cool on a rack. For crispier loaves, put them on a baking sheet and return to the oven for an additional 5 minutes.

MAKES 4 LOAVES

. . . .

Smoked Trout Mousse on Toast Points

Apples and radishes would be tangy additions to this mousse, which can be made with other smoked fish if a good smoked trout is not available.

- **1 medium-size smoked trout**
- **2 teaspoons finely minced fresh horseradish**
- **1½ to 2 tablespoons freshly squeezed lemon juice**
- **1½ teaspoons finely grated lemon rind**
- **Dash of cayenne pepper**
- **Salt and freshly ground white pepper, to taste**
- **1 cup heavy cream, whipped**
- **2 medium radishes, finely minced (optional)**
- **2 tablespoons peeled, minced Granny Smith or Pippin apples (optional)**
- **8 to 16 slices bakery-quality white or whole wheat bread**

Remove the head and tail from the trout and discard. Carefully remove the skin and bones. You should have about 1 cup of trout meat.

Put the trout in a food processor fitted with the steel blade and process just until finely minced. Do not overprocess. Mix in the horseradish, lemon juice, lemon rind, cayenne pepper, salt, and white pepper. Gently fold in the whipped cream, and radish and apple, if desired. Taste and adjust seasonings, if necessary. Mound the mousse on a serving dish and chill overnight to blend the flavors and firm up the consistency.

To make toast points, remove the crusts from freshly made toast and slice each piece on the diagonal into 2 or 4 pieces. Serve with the mousse.

SERVES 12 OR MORE

. . . .

Currant Scones

A quite proper tea can consist of no more than freshly made scones with butter or jam and thick cream—Devonshire in England, crème fraîche in France. This is the classical recipe for scones, but they can be varied with chopped nuts, raisins, or dates.

3	cups unbleached all-purpose flour
½	cup sugar
½	teaspoon salt
½	teaspoon baking soda
1	cup (2 sticks) unsalted butter, at room temperature
2	tablespoons vegetable shortening
½	cup dried currants
2	eggs, beaten
2	tablespoons buttermilk (or substitute sour cream, plain yogurt, or reconstituted dried buttermilk)

Preheat the oven to 350°. Grease and lightly flour 2 baking sheets.

In a mixing bowl, combine the flour, sugar, salt, and baking soda. Add the butter and vegetable shortening, and mix to a coarse grain with a pastry blender or your fingertips. Stir in the currants. Add the eggs and buttermilk and stir just until the mixture forms a dough. Using a spoon drop 9 to 12 mounds of dough (depending on the desired size) onto each baking sheet, and lightly press each mound with a fork. Bake for 12 to 15 minutes, until lightly brown around the edges. Serve warm with unsalted butter, Lemon Maple Marmalade, or Rhubarb Conserve (recipes follow), and/or lightly sweetened whipped cream.

MAKES 18 TO 24 SCONES

Rhubarb Conserve

Unusual, simple, tart-sweet, and very pretty.

1	orange (unpeeled)
1	lemon (unpeeled)
2	whole cloves
½	cup water
¼	cup distilled vinegar
1½	cups rhubarb, either strawberry or cherry (see Note), trimmed and cut into 1-inch lengths
3	cups sugar

Cut the orange and lemon into very thin slices, remove the seeds, and cut the slices in half. Put the slices in a heavy enameled or stainless steel pan. Add the cloves and cover with the water and vinegar. Simmer, uncovered, for 15 minutes, until the fruit is tender.

Add the rhubarb and sugar and slowly bring to a boil, mixing well. Reduce the heat and simmer very slowly, uncovered, stirring occasionally, until thick. This may take up to 45 minutes. Remove the cloves.

Refrigerate, unsealed, for up to 3 weeks, or ladle into hot, sterilized jars to within ¼ inch of the top and seal immediately with paraffin, or sterile two-piece lids if canning jars are used. When cool, store in a cool, dark place.

NOTE: Strawberry rhubarb, which is hothouse-grown, is bright red to pink, and milder in flavor than cherry rhubarb, which is field-grown and dark red to greenish. Strawberry rhubarb is available from late January to the end of March in California, while cherry rhubarb is grown from April to October.

MAKES APPROXIMATELY 3½ CUPS

Lemon-Maple Marmalade

This is an interesting variation of the more traditional orange marmalade. Make sure to use only the best-quality pure maple syrup.

> 5 **lemons (approximately)**
> 4 **cups water**
> 4 **cups sugar**
> 1 **tablespoon maple syrup**

Wash but do not peel the lemons. Thinly slice, then seed. Cut the slices into quarters. You should have 4 cups. In a heavy saucepan, cover the lemon slices with the water and let stand overnight.

Without draining, bring the lemon and water mixture to a boil and simmer, uncovered, for 20 to 30 minutes, until the rind is soft. Add the sugar, bring to a boil, reduce the heat, and simmer until the temperature reaches 220° to 222° on a candy thermometer. Remove from the heat and stir gently to distribute the fruit. Add the maple syrup and blend well.

Refrigerate, unsealed, for up to 3 weeks, or ladle into hot, sterilized jars to within ¼ inch of the top and seal immediately with paraffin, or sterile two-piece lids if canning jars are used. When cool, store in a cool, dark place.

MAKES 4 TO 5 CUPS

. . . .

Frangipani Tartlets

There was a sixteenth-century Italian Marquis Frangipani who invented perfume, but how or why his name was given to a pastry made of ground almonds is not clear. It doesn't matter; these tartlets are excellent, rich but not too sweet. They may be frozen either before or after baking.

PASTRY

> 2½ **cups sifted unbleached all-purpose flour**
> 3 **tablespoons sugar**
> 12 **tablespoons (1½ sticks) unsalted butter, at room temperature**
> 3 **hard-cooked egg yolks, mashed or sieved**
> 2 **raw egg yolks**
> ½ **teaspoon salt**
> 2 **teaspoons grated lemon rind**

A sweet wine is perfect with a selection of sweets (above). Coffee accompanies a generous slice of chocolate-mocha torte.

FRANGIPANI FILLING
MAKES 2 CUPS

- 8 ounces almond paste, at room temperature (see Note)
- 8 tablespoons (1 stick) unsalted butter, at room temperature, cut into several pieces
- 2 eggs, beaten
- 2 teaspoons grated lemon rind
- 2 teaspoons unbleached all-purpose flour
- ¼ teaspoon salt
- ¾ cup sugar
- 1½ teaspoons almond extract
- ½ teaspoon lemon extract

GARNISH
- 60 pieces of assorted fruit, such as sliced kumquats, raspberries, blackberries, and strawberries
- 1 10-ounce jar of red currant jam, melted and cooled
  Confectioners' sugar, sifted

To make the pastry, put the flour in a mound on a worktable or in a bowl. Make a well in the center and put the rest of the pastry ingredients in the well. Working quickly, using just your fingertips, make a paste of the center ingredients, gradually blending in more and more flour to make a firm ball. Wrap the dough in plastic wrap and chill for at least 1 hour.

To make the filling, put the almond paste in a food processor fitted with the steel blade and process until uniform and crumbly. With the machine running, add the butter piece by piece through the feed tube and process until smooth. Add the eggs in a slow steady stream. Then add the lemon rind, flour, salt, sugar, and extracts. Process until well blended and set aside.

Roll out the pastry between pieces of plastic wrap or wax paper to a thickness of ⅛ inch. Using a biscuit cutter, cut the dough into circles slightly larger than miniature muffin tins or 3-inch tartlet pans, and gently ease it into the pans, which need not be greased. Chill or freeze the pastry shells for 1 hour or more.

Preheat the oven to 350°. Fill the pastry shells three quarters full with the frangipani filling. Bake in the lower third of the oven for 15 to 20 minutes, until the filling is set. Do not overbake. Let cool on racks.

If desired, top with sliced kumquats, raspberries, blackberries, or strawberries and brush with red current glaze, or dust with confectioners' sugar.

NOTE: Almond paste sometimes comes in a 7-ounce package. If you use this amount, reduce the butter in the filling by 1 tablespoon.

MAKES ABOUT SIXTY MINIATURE OR THIRTY 3-INCH TARTLETS

Chocolate-Mocha Torte

Chocolate and coffee are an irresistible combination. Be sure to use the best-quality imported chocolate for this lovely little torte.

- ⅜ **cup water**
- 1½ **tablespoons instant espresso coffee powder**
- ¾ **cup (4½ ounces) good quality**
  semisweet or bittersweet chocolate
- 10 **eggs, separated**
- ¾ **cup sugar**
- 8 **tablespoons (1 stick) unsalted butter,**
  at room temperature, cut into pieces
- ¾ **cup unbleached all-purpose flour**
- ½ **teaspoon cream of tartar**

F R O S T I N G
- 12 **ounces good quality semisweet or**
  bittersweet chocolate
- 1 **cup (2 sticks) unsalted butter**
- 1 **cup sifted confectioners' sugar**
- 2 **tablespoons instant espresso coffee powder**
- 4 **egg yolks, beaten**
- 6 **tablespoons heavy cream**
- 2 **teaspoons vanilla extract**

G A R N I S H
Chocolate coffee beans

Preheat the oven to 325°. Grease and flour the bottoms of six 8-inch cake pans. Line them with wax paper or parchment paper which has been greased and floured.

Combine the water and instant coffee, bring to a boil, reduce the heat, and add the chocolate. Cook, stirring, until the chocolate melts and the mixture is smooth. Let cool slightly.

Beat the egg yolks with the sugar until thick and pale lemon in color. Add the butter and beat until smooth. Add the slightly cooled chocolate mixture and beat until creamy. Fold in the flour.

Beat the egg whites with the cream of tartar until soft peaks form. Stir a third of the egg whites into the chocolate mixture, then gently fold in the rest. Divide the batter among the prepared pans, using about 1 cup for each. Bake for 15 minutes in the lower third of the oven. Let cool in the pans for 5 minutes. Remove the layers from the pans while hot and invert onto racks. Peel off the paper immediately and let cool thoroughly.

To make the frosting, melt the chocolate and butter together over hot water. Mix the sugar and coffee and gradually stir into the chocolate. Add the egg yolks, cream, and vanilla and beat until smooth and creamy. Chill until the frosting is of good spreading consistency.

Frost the torte between the layers, on top, and around the sides. Decorate the top with chocolate coffee beans.

M A K E S   O N E   8 - I N C H   T O R T E

A pinwheel of shortbread cookies.

Chocolate-Dipped Shortbread Cookies

This shortbread would be good by itself, but it is certainly more decorative for the tea table when dipped in chocolate and topped with an almond.

- 1 **pound (4 sticks) unsalted butter, at**
  room temperature
- 1 **cup plus 2 tablespoons sugar**
- 5 **cups unbleached all-purpose flour**
  Large pinch of salt

C H O C O L A T E   G L A Z E
- 9 **ounces good quality bittersweet or**
  semisweet chocolate, cut into small pieces
- 6 **tablespoons (¾ stick) unsalted butter**

- 45 **or more whole blanched almonds**

Preheat the oven to 250°. Lightly butter the bottom and sides of a 10½ × 15½-inch jelly roll pan.

Beat the butter and sugar together until fluffy and pale in color. Gradually add the flour and salt, and mix until the dough comes together into a ball. Press the dough firmly into the pan.

Bake for approximately 2 hours, until just starting to turn a light golden brown. Remove from the oven. With a very sharp knife, immediately cut into 1 × 3-inch rectangles and let cool in the pan for 10 to 15 minutes. Transfer the cookies to a rack to continue cooling.

To make the glaze, melt together the chocolate and butter and let cool slightly. Brush off crumbs from each shortbread cookie and, holding it lengthwise, carefully dip one third into the glaze. Hold up for a few seconds over wax paper to let the chocolate drip off. Place an almond in the center of each glazed edge, then place on wax paper until the chocolate is set. Store in an airtight container.

MAKES 45 OR MORE COOKIES

. . . .

Citrus Pecans

A California version of the praline, these are popular with guests who have a sweet tooth.

    3 cups sugar
    1 cup water
    4 cups whole pecans
    ½ cup grated orange rind, or a combination
       of orange and lemon rind

Combine the sugar and water in a saucepan. Stir over low heat until the sugar dissolves. Increase the heat to medium high, bring to a boil, and continue cooking, *without stirring*, until the temperature reaches 240° on a candy thermometer.

Remove from the heat and stir in the pecans and orange rind. Stir until the syrup become cloudy. Quickly turn the mixture out onto wax paper. Separate into clusters or individual nuts before they are completely hardened. Store in an airtight container.

MAKES 4 CUPS

Caraway Cake

A light and simple cake flavored with caraway seeds and a hint of mace. The glaze makes it pretty enough for the tea table.

    1 cup (2 sticks) unsalted butter, at room
       temperature
  1⅔ cups sugar
    1 teaspoon vanilla extract
    ¼ teaspoon mace
  2⅔ cups sifted cake flour
    8 egg whites, at room temperature
    ½ teaspoon cream of tartar
    ¼ teaspoon salt
    3 tablespoons caraway seeds

GLAZE
  1½ cups sifted confectioners' sugar
    2 tablespoons hot milk
    ¾ teaspoon vanilla extract

Preheat the oven to 350°. Grease and flour a 10-inch bundt or tube pan and set aside.

In a mixing bowl, cream the butter, gradually adding ⅔ cup sugar, and beat until creamy. Add the vanilla and mace and continue mixing. Gradually beat in 1⅔ cups of the sifted cake flour.

In another bowl, beat the egg whites with the cream of tartar and salt until foamy. Gradually add the remaining 1 cup sugar and continue beating until the egg whites are stiff. Add a quarter of the egg white mixture to the batter and mix thoroughly with a wooden spoon. Fold the batter into the remaining egg whites and sprinkle with the remaining 1 cup flour. Gently fold the caraway seeds into the mixture, being careful not to overmix. Pour the batter into the prepared pan. Bake for 45 minutes, or until a toothpick comes out dry. Let cool in the pan for 15 minutes and carefully turn out onto a rack to cool completely.

To make the glaze, mix the confectioners' sugar, hot milk, and vanilla in a small bowl. Pour over the top of the cooled cake, letting some run down unevenly on the sides. Cut the cake into thin slices and serve.

MAKES ONE 10-INCH CAKE

Glazed caraway cake, a rich mocha torte, and fresh cherries.

MOUNTAINS

The strategically positioned mountains of California have been as important as the ocean in influencing California lifestyles. They keep the fiery temperatures of the desert in their place, protect the great agricultural plains, and intervene between the fury of ocean winds and the delicate vegetation of the coastal valleys.

The Coast range runs an irregular way along the Pacific, enclosing and protecting innumerable small, fertile valleys; vineyards in the Napa Valley climb the slopes of the Mayacama mountains. Along the eastern border, the magnificent Sierra Nevadas rise to the highest point in the United States (excluding Alaska). The two ranges come together in the north, and are joined in the south by the Tehachapis, thus walling in the great central valley.

In California everyone lives within sight of the mountains. The Santa Monicas neatly bisect the city of Los Angeles. The San Gabriels and the San Bernardinos majestically guard the horizon on a clear day, and Tamalpais is just across the bay from San Francisco.

Everyone goes to the mountains—for solace, for silence, for play, for reassurance. They are beautiful. They contain us. Without them, California would be a desert.

SANTA YNEZ VALLEY

Waverley Root was fond of saying that the best cooking is found in the areas that grow wine grapes. And this is certainly true in California. Although Napa Valley is the historic wine country, blessed with everything it needs—soil, climate, the tempering sea with mountains to filter the breezes—medal-winning wines are now being made in other places.

''Pockets'' is the cryptic answer when one asks about the wines in the Santa Ynez Valley, for example. It means simply that in areas generally considered unfavorable to grapes, there may be some parts—pockets—where an angle of mountains, a ricochet of sea breeze, and the right kind of soil have somehow established the proper conditions. The Pinot Noirs from the Santa Ynez Valley are splendid. So are the Chardonnays and Cabernet Sauvignons.

Even before wines, the Santa Ynez Valley was a dream of country living. Mountains face the sea in a great horseshoe. There are big, tawny ranches, and horses for riding. Small villages nestled at the crossroads still seem to be waiting for the next stagecoach.

For a contemporary food lover, this vineyard-ranch is a paradise. The trout for breakfast were freshly caught that morning. There are quail, and doves, and apples from the trees. Sage grows wild, and rosemary is there for the picking. Squash and pumpkin come from the garden. The sausage was made of wild boar from the ranch—the recipe has been changed to pork for those who do not have a wild boar roaming the hills.

The guests rode horses through the vineyards and up the mountain trails before breakfast, ready for them under a tree when they returned. Dinner was formally served in the winery, the wines selected by the winemaker from his own best vintages.

BREAKFAST AFTER THE RIDE

FOR **12**

Whole Wheat Apple Pancakes

Trout with Grape-Almond Stuffing

Twice-Cooked Potato Patties

Sage Sausage Cakes

Freshly Squeezed Orange Juice

Rosé of Cabernet Sauvignon

. . . .

The hearty country breakfast of stuffed trout, pancakes, and sausage is cooked on the grill (above) and served on old-fashioned blue enamel plates.

Whole Wheat Apple Pancakes

The Indians made pancakes from cornmeal, the Dutch from buckwheat, and the Germans probably added apples. Whatever, pancakes have been made in this country in various ways since the beginning. Several traditions are happily combined in these whole wheat hearties.

⅔ **cup old-fashioned rolled oats**
1⅓ **cups whole wheat flour**
⅔ **cup unbleached all-purpose flour**
⅔ **cup yellow cornmeal**
4 **teaspoons baking powder**
2 **teaspoons baking soda**
2 **teaspoons salt**
¾ **cup (1½ sticks) unsalted butter, chilled and cut into bits**
4 **cups buttermilk**
4 **eggs, lightly beaten**
6 **tablespoons brown sugar**
1 **teaspoon cinnamon**
3 **cups (about 2 large) Golden Delicious apples, peeled, cored, and sliced or chopped**
  Clarified butter (see Note) or vegetable oil

In a food processor fitted with the steel blade, process the oats to a coarse powder. Transfer to a large bowl. Add the flours, cornmeal, baking powder, baking soda, and salt and combine well. Using your fingertips or a pastry blender, blend in the butter until the mixture resembles coarse meal.

In another bowl, combine the buttermilk, eggs, brown sugar, and cinnamon. Add this mixture to the flour mixture and stir just until combined. Stir in the apples and let the batter stand for 5 minutes. Thin with a little milk, if necessary.

Preheat the oven to the lowest setting. Heat a large pan or griddle over moderately high heat and brush with clarified butter or oil. Pour in the batter to make pancakes that spread to about 4 inches in diameter. Cook for 2 to 3 minutes to brown the underside. When the top is bubbly, turn and finish cooking the other side. Transfer the pancakes to an ovenproof dish and keep warm in the oven. Continue to make pancakes with the remaining batter. Serve hot, with maple syrup or a berry syrup on the side.

NOTE: To clarify butter, melt it over low heat and skim off the foam that forms on the surface. Spoon the clear liquid—the clarified butter—into another container, and discard the milky residue at the bottom of the pan.

MAKES 40 TO 48 PANCAKES

Breakfast After the Ride **187**

A stack of baled straw is background for a wooden trough filled with barbecued trout and wine grapes. The wine cools in an ice-filled wooden bowl (top). A sun-dappled table looks especially inviting after a brisk ride (above).

Trout with Grape-Almond Stuffing

Wrapping the trout in grape leaves adds the flavor of the vineyard and contains the juices.

12 fresh trout, 6 to 8 ounces each, boned and cleaned, heads and tails left on
3 to 4 dozen large grape or Boston lettuce leaves
    Salt and freshly ground black pepper, to taste

GRAPE-ALMOND STUFFING

8 tablespoons (1 stick) unsalted butter
3 cups diced bread cubes, made from white bread slices with crusts removed
1 cup seedless grapes, quartered
½ cup chopped blanched almonds (or substitute walnuts or pecans)
1 teaspoon salt
½ teaspoon paprika
1 tablespoon grated lemon rind

GARNISH

Lemon wedges

Wash and dry the trout, then refrigerate until ready to stuff. In boiling water, parboil the grape leaves for 10 seconds or lettuce leaves for 3 seconds. Drain and set aside.

Prepare a barbecue grill or preheat the oven to 450°.

Melt the butter in a skillet and sauté the bread cubes until lightly toasted. Remove from the heat and mix in the remaining ingredients. Sprinkle the cavity of each trout with salt and pepper, and stuff with approximately ⅓ cup of the stuffing.

Wrap the grape or lettuce leaves around the trout, making sure to cover the open side securely, and wrap in heavy aluminum foil. Barbecue or bake in the oven for 12 to 15 minutes, until the fish test done. Remove the foil and grape or lettuce leaves and serve immediately, garnished with lemon wedges.

SERVES 12

Twice-Cooked Potato Patties

Parboiling the potatoes make peeling easier, and also means that the patties can be shaped in advance without turning brown.

2½ to 3 pounds potatoes, unpeeled
¼ cup chopped onion
¼ cup chopped pimiento
¼ cup chopped fresh parsley
¼ cup (or more) unbleached all-purpose flour
2 teaspoons salt
6 to 8 tablespoons unsalted butter

Parboil the potatoes for 15 to 20 minutes in boiling salted water. (They will still be hard at the center.) Cool under running water. Peel, and shred with a coarse grater. Lightly toss with the onion, pimiento, parsley, flour, and salt. Shape into 12 patties, using ½ cup for each, adding more flour, if necessary, to hold the patties together.

Heat the butter in a large skillet and brown the potato patties in batches for 6 to 8 minutes on each side. Drain and serve immediately.

MAKES 12 PATTIES

Sage Sausage Cakes

The sausages in the photograph were made with wild boar from the ranch and stuffed into casings. These, made of pork, are a very good substitute.

1½ pounds boneless pork shoulder, coarsely ground
½ pound fresh pork fat, ground
1 teaspoon salt
1 tablespoon crushed sage
½ teaspoon allspice
    Freshly ground black pepper, to taste

Combine all ingredients in a mixing bowl and refrigerate overnight.

Sauté a bit of the mixture in a hot frying pan and taste for seasonings. Form into 2½-inch patties. In a large pan over moderate heat, sauté the sausage cakes for 6 minutes on each side, until well browned. Make sure the pork is well cooked. Drain and serve immediately.

NOTE: Sausage cakes may also be barbecued.

MAKES 12 SAUSAGE CAKES

WINERY DINNER

FOR **6**

Squab, Apple, and Walnut Timbales with
Pinot Noir Sauce

White Wine Sorbet

Rack of Lamb with Mustard and Herbs

Puréed Carrots in Squash Cups   **P**otato Gratin

Pumpkin Mousse in Brandy Snap Baskets

W I N E S :

Full-Bodied Chardonnay or Gamay with Timbales

Aged Cabernet Sauvignon with Lamb

. . . .

Pinot noir grapes grown on the ranch.

Squab, Apple, and Walnut Timbales with Pinot Noir Sauce

A pretty dish to set before a king—or a wine lover, who will appreciate the rich sauce on the flavorful timbales. The sauce would also be excellent on plain broiled squab or quail.

½ medium garlic clove
¾ pound boned skinned squab (about 2 to 3 squabs), or substitute chicken thighs
1 egg
¼ cup heavy cream
¼ teaspoon salt
¼ teaspoon freshly ground white pepper
1 Pippin apple, peeled, cored, and diced
1½ tablespoons unsalted butter
¼ cup chopped walnuts
12 medium to large preserved grape leaves, stems removed, rinsed, blanched, and dried (see Note)

PINOT NOIR SAUCE

3 tablespoons minced shallots
1½ tablespoons unsalted butter
¾ cup Pinot Noir
2¼ cups chicken stock, preferably homemade (page 17)
¾ cup heavy cream

GARNISH

Thin slices of unpeeled green apples
Chopped walnuts

With the machine running, drop the garlic through the feed tube of a food processor fitted with the steel blade. Add the squab and process until finely minced. Add the egg, heavy cream, salt, and pepper and process until smooth. Transfer the mixture to a bowl. Sauté the apple in the butter until soft, and add to the squab mixture. Stir in the walnuts and set the mixture aside.

Preheat oven to 350° and oil six 3-inch ramekins.

In each ramekin arrange 2 grape leaves, stem side up and underside facing in, leaving enough of the leaf at the top to cover the squab mixture completely. Spoon the squab mixture into the leaf-lined ramekins and fold the top of the leaves over to completely encase the filling. Flatten each timbale with your fingers, and cover with aluminum foil.

Place the ramekins in a pan, and pour in boiling water to reach halfway up the sides of the ramekins. Bake for 40 minutes.

While the timbales are baking, prepare the sauce. Sauté the shallots in the butter until softened. Add the Pinot Noir and reduce to 2 tablespoons. Add the chicken stock and reduce by half. Add the cream and reduce by half again.

Just before the timbales are done, arrange green apple slices on individual plates. Unmold the timbales, place on top of the apple slices, and spoon on some of the Pinot Noir sauce. Sprinkle with walnuts.

NOTE: If available, use fresh grape leaves. Cook them in boiling water for 2 to 3 minutes, until softened.

SERVES 6

Grapeleaf-wrapped timbales, crowned with Pinot Noir sauce, sit on green apple slices.

White wine sorbet looks dainty in fluted glass.

White Wine Sorbet

Sorbets were originally intended as a period of grace and a palate cleanser between the entrée and the roast in those interminable dinners people used to eat. On a modern menu, they can be refreshing when, as here, meat follows a fowl. This sorbet is best eaten the same day it is made.

¾	cup sugar
1½	cups water
1	1-inch piece of vanilla bean
	Peel of 1 orange
	Peel of 1 lemon
2	cups Chardonnay or other dry white wine
	Strained juice of 2 oranges
	Strained juice of 1 lemon

GARNISH
 Orange peel cutouts

In a medium saucepan dissolve the sugar in the water. Add the vanilla bean, orange peel, and lemon peel and simmer for 15 minutes. Let cool. Remove the vanilla bean and citrus peels. Add the wine, orange juice, and lemon juice. Pour into a shallow ice tray and freeze.

When the mixture begins to freeze around the edges, stir to break up the crystals. Repeat this procedure every hour for 3 or 4 hours of freezing. When frozen, process until smooth in a food processor fitted with the steel blade. Serve immediately, garnished with orange peel cutouts, or refreeze until serving time.

SERVES 6

Rack of Lamb with Mustard and Herbs

Here as in the wine country of Bordeaux, the mustard, the herbs, and the oil enrich and flavor a fine rack of lamb. The crumb coating quickly forms a crust when placed in a hot oven.

MUSTARD-HERB COATING

3	tablespoons Dijon-style mustard
2	tablespoons olive oil
4	garlic cloves, crushed
½	teaspoon dried oregano
½	teaspoon dried thyme
½	teaspoon dried rosemary
	Salt and freshly ground black pepper, to taste
2	racks of lamb (8 or 9 chops each), trimmed and frenched

CRUMB COATING

¾	cup unsalted butter
¼	cup minced shallots
4	garlic cloves, minced
2	cups dry bread crumbs
¼	cup minced fresh parsley
1	teaspoon dried thyme
1	teaspoon dried rosemary

GARNISH
 Fresh rosemary

Combine the mustard-herb coating ingredients and rub over the lamb. Let sit, covered, overnight in the refrigerator.

Preheat the oven to 500°. To make the crumb coating, melt the butter in a skillet. Sauté the shallots and garlic until softened. Add the bread crumbs, parsley, thyme, and rosemary and heat through, stirring, for 1 or 2 minutes.

Place the lamb, fat side up, in a heavy roasting pan and roast for 10 minutes. Remove the pan from the oven and pat the crumb mixture firmly onto the lamb. Reduce the oven to 400° and return the lamb to the oven for another 12 minutes. Cover the rib bones with aluminum foil if they begin to brown too much. The meat should be medium rare. Slice through individual chops and put 2 on each plate. Garnish with fresh rosemary, if desired, and serve immediately.

SERVES 6

Puréed Carrots in Squash Cups

Puréed vegetables are a contemporary flourish and this is a pretty way to serve them. The squash cups may be assembled a day ahead and baked just before serving.

- **6 pattypan squash (approximately 2½ inches in diameter), trimmed**
- **1½ pounds carrots, peeled and cut into ½-inch pieces**
- **3 tablespoons unsalted butter, at room temperature**
  Salt and freshly ground white pepper, to taste
- **2 to 3 teaspoons chopped fresh dill**
  Unsalted butter, melted

With a melon baller, scoop out the top of each squash, being careful not to pierce the bottom. Set aside.

Cook the carrots in boiling salted water for 15 to 20 minutes, until tender. Drain well. Purée the carrots with 3 tablespoons butter in a food processor fitted with the steel blade. Add salt and pepper and dill.

Preheat the oven to 350° and oil a baking sheet. Using a pastry bag fitted with a star tip (or a spoon), pipe the purée into the squash cups. Brush with melted butter and bake, covered with aluminum foil, on the baking sheet for about 30 minutes. Serve hot.

S E R V E S 6

. . . .

Potato Gratin

A fine and simple way to serve potatoes. Putting the slices in cold water not only keeps them white, but also removes starch that would cause them to stick together in an unlovely clump.

- **1 medium garlic clove, unpeeled and halved**
- **4 tablespoons (½ stick) unsalted butter**
- **3 pounds boiling potatoes**
- **1 teaspoon salt**
  Freshly ground black pepper, to taste
- **1½ cups milk**

Preheat the oven to 425°. Rub a 12-inch gratin pan or similar dish with the cut garlic and 1 tablespoon butter.

Peel the potatoes and slice approximately ⅛ inch thick. Place in cold water. When ready to bake, drain the potatoes and dry with a towel. Spread half the potatoes in the bottom of the pan and season with ½ teaspoon salt, pepper, and 1½ tablespoons butter. Arrange the remaining potatoes over the first layer and season with the remaining salt, pepper, and butter.

Bring the milk to a boil and pour over the potatoes. Place the gratin pan on the stove and bring the milk to a simmer (eliminate this step if your gratin pan is not flameproof), then place in the oven. Bake for about 30 minutes, until the potatoes are tender, the milk has been absorbed, and the top is nicely browned. Serve immediately, or keep warm in the turned-off oven for up to 40 minutes.

S E R V E S 6

The lamb is rare, the squash cups are bright, and the wine is special.

Pumpkin Mousse in Brandy Snap Baskets

A suitably indulgent finish to a special dinner, the mousse would also be fine for the holidays.

PUMPKIN MOUSSE

- 1 envelope unflavored gelatin
- ¼ cup cold water
- 3 eggs, at room temperature, separated
- ½ cup sugar
- 1¼ cups puréed pumpkin
- ½ teaspoon ground ginger
- ½ teaspoon ground cinnamon
- ½ teaspoon ground nutmeg
- ¼ teaspoon salt
- ½ cup milk
- ½ cup heavy cream

BRANDY SNAP BASKETS

- 8 tablespoons (1 stick) unsalted butter
- ½ cup sugar
- ⅓ cup dark molasses
- ¼ teaspoon ground ginger
- ½ teaspoon ground cinnamon
- 1 teaspoon grated orange rind
- ¾ cup plus 1 tablespoon unbleached all-purpose flour
- 2 tablespoons brandy

GARNISH

- Orange peel slices
- Whipped cream
- Candied violets or crystallized ginger

To make the mousse, soften the gelatin in the cold water. In a heavy saucepan, beat the egg yolks with sugar until thick and pale yellow. Add the pumpkin, ginger, cinnamon, nutmeg, salt, and milk. Cook the mixture, stirring, for 3 to 5 minutes, until thickened. Add the gelatin and stir until dissolved. Remove from the heat and let cool. Whip the cream and set it aside. Whip the egg whites just until they hold their shape, and fold into pumpkin mixture along with the whipped cream. Chill for 4 to 6 hours, until set.

To make brandy snap baskets, preheat the oven to 300°. Combine the butter, sugar, molasses, ginger, cinnamon, and orange rind in a saucepan and heat until the butter melts. Remove from the heat and stir in the flour, then the brandy. Mix until smooth.

For each basket, drop about 1½ tablespoons of the batter onto an ungreased baking sheet. The batter will spread considerably, so make only 2 to 3 cookies per sheet. Bake for 18 to 20 minutes. The centers will still be soft, but the cookies will harden as they rest. Let the cookies rest for 30 to 60 seconds, then remove from the baking sheet with a spatula and shape into a cup over the bottom of a glass or custard cup. Do not prepare more than one sheet of cookies at a time, or they will harden before they can be shaped into baskets. Prepare 6 to 8 baskets (see Note). Store the baskets in an airtight container and use within a day, or freeze.

To assemble, spoon the chilled pumpkin mixture into the brandy snap baskets. Make a handle from a ¼-inch slice of orange peel, and tuck the edges into the brandy basket. Garnish with additional whipped cream and crystallized ginger or candied violets, if desired.

NOTE: Leftover dough may be made as above, or the cookies may be rolled up tightly like a cigar.

SERVES 6 TO 8

Brandy snap cups filled with pumpkin mousse look especially festive on these antique Venetian glass fluted plates.

LAKE TAHOE

Lake Tahoe is the most important and the most beautiful lake in California. Located more than 6,000 feet above sea level in the magnificent Sierra Nevadas, it is deeply, brilliantly blue, like an extraordinary sapphire. Popular both winter and summer, it could be a symbol of active California. The ski runs in the adjacent Squaw Valley are superlative—the Winter Olympics were held there in 1960. There is excellent cross-country skiing, ice skating, and snowmobiling. In summer water skiing, sailing, tennis, and golf abound.

It was summer and a gathering of friends who love to cruise Lake Tahoe in classic wooden boats—there are those who collect classic boats and those who collect classic cars—prompted this buffet on a dock. The flank steaks had been flavored in their marinade and were ready for the grill, as were the leeks. The chili was carried from the house in a great pot. Beer and wine were on ice in a foil-lined basket.

At the southern end of Tahoe are two smaller lakes, so small they scarcely show on the map, as though they were drops flicked from God's fingers when He finished brimming the blue water in the big lake and stood back to judge the effect. Narrow, pathlike roads lead to these little lakes, pristine with trees down to the shore and only a few cabins tucked among them. Dinner was served in one of these cabins, as comfortable as home, with the table pulled close to the fire. Pot roast was the stalwart fare needed after an active day. The beef, brightened with green olives, wine, and fresh basil, was served from its pot and accompanied by orzo, rice-shaped pasta from Greece (although buttered noodles could have been substituted). Hot bloody marys in mugs were warming potions for guests on the porch while the sun went down. Then it became suddenly very cold in the mountains, and the fire was welcome and wonderful.

FIRESIDE DINNER

FOR **8**

Hot Bloody Marys

Sautéed Carrots with Thyme

Pot Roast with Olives

Orzo or Buttered Noodles

Walnut Spice Cake with Brandy Buttercream

Ice-Cold Beer

Barbera or Zinfandel

. . . .

Hearty mountain fare is served on specially designed, handmade plates with reindeer ambling along the rims.

Hot Bloody Marys

Actually, this is spicy tomato soup. The 10-minute simmer will evaporate the alcohol, leaving only the flavor of the vodka. If vodka is wanted as vodka, add it only a few seconds before the soup comes off the fire.

- 1 46-ounce can of tomato or vegetable cocktail juice
- 1 cup freshly squeezed orange juice
  Juice of 3 lemons
- 3 tablespoons crushed dried tarragon
- 2 tablespoons sugar
- 1 teaspoon coarse salt
- 2 teaspoons freshly ground black pepper
  Dash of Tabasco sauce
- 1 cup vodka, or more to taste (optional)

GARNISH

Chopped celery and scallions, or celery stalks and tomato slices

Combine all the ingredients and bring to a boil. Reduce the heat and simmer for 10 minutes. Taste for seasonings. Serve hot, in bowls, garnished with chopped celery and scallions, or in mugs, garnished with a stalk of celery and a slice of tomato. If desired, serve with Black Bread (page 209) and unsalted butter.

SERVES 8

. . . .

Sautéed Carrots with Thyme

Carrots cooked this way are fresh and colorful—a nice alternative to the mushy carrots commonly found with pot roast.

- 2 pounds carrots, peeled and sliced
  ¼ inch thick on the diagonal
- 3 tablespoons unsalted butter
- 1 teaspoon vegetable oil
- 3 tablespoons finely minced shallots
- 1 large garlic clove, minced
- 3 tablespoons finely minced fresh parsley
- 1½ teaspoons fresh thyme or ¾ teaspoon dried
  Salt and freshly ground black pepper, to taste

Steam the carrots over boiling water for about 5 minutes, until barely tender. Drain well and set aside. Heat the butter and oil in a skillet over medium heat. Sauté the shallots for 3 to 4 minutes, until softened. Add the garlic and sauté for 1 minute more. Dry the carrots well and add to the pan, along with the parsley, thyme, salt, and pepper, and heat through for about 3 minutes, stirring occasionally. Serve immediately.

SERVES 8

Pot Roast with Olives

Green olives, green or red pepper, basil, and wine lift this pot roast well out of the ordinary. It can be made ahead—all the better for a bit of mellowing.

- 5 to 6 pounds boneless chuck roast, wiped dry with paper towels
  Unbleached all-purpose flour
- 2 to 3 tablespoons olive or vegetable oil
- 2 medium garlic cloves, crushed
- 2 teaspoons salt
- 1 cup dry bread crumbs
- ½ cup minced fresh parsley
- 8 tablespoons (1 stick) unsalted butter, melted
- 1 green or red bell pepper, chopped
- 1 cup Spanish green olives with pimientos
- 12 to 18 pearl onions, peeled (see Note)
- ¼ cup finely chopped fresh basil leaves, or 1½ tablespoons dried
- ¾ to 1 bottle dry red wine
- 2 ounces brandy (optional)

Preheat the oven to 325°. Flour the roast and brown it in the oil over medium high heat. Spread the crushed garlic on the browned roast. Sprinkle with salt. Mix the bread crumbs with the minced parsley and melted butter and spread on top of the meat. Place the roast in a large, covered casserole and add the chopped green or red pepper, stuffed olives, onions, and basil. Pour in the wine and add the brandy, if used. Bake, covered, for 4 or more hours, until the meat is tender. Make sure the liquid is always kept at a simmer. Remove the cover for the last ½ hour or so to reduce the liquid and brown the meat a little.

Remove the roast from the oven and degrease the pan juices. Slice the roast and serve on a heated platter with the pan juices.

N O T E : To peel pearl onions, cut off the tops and tails, submerge in a pot of boiling water for about 10 seconds, then place under cold running water. Remove the skins and the slippery membrane underneath.

S E R V E S 8

· · · · · · · · · · · · · · · · ·

Walnut Spice Cake with Brandy Buttercream

A fine, long-lasting cake, almost a torte, made mostly with eggs and nuts. It will keep for a week in the refrigerator, and also freezes nicely.

- 3 cups (about 12 ounces) walnuts, finely ground
- ½ cup fine dry bread crumbs
- 1 tablespoon grated orange rind
- 2 teaspoons grated lemon rind
- 2 teaspoons baking powder
- 1 teaspoon ground cinnamon
- 1 teaspoon ground cloves
- ½ teaspoon salt
- 9 eggs, at room temperature, separated
- 1 cup sugar
- 1 teaspoon vanilla extract
- ½ cup water
- ¼ teaspoon cream of tartar

B R A N D Y B U T T E R C R E A M

- 6 tablespoons (¾ stick) unsalted butter, at room temperature
- 2½ cups confectioners' sugar, sifted
  Pinch of salt
- 1 egg
- ¾ teaspoon vanilla extract
- 1½ tablespoons (or more) brandy

G A R N I S H
Walnut halves

Grease three 8-inch round cake pans, line them with wax paper, and grease the paper. Set aside. Preheat the oven to 350°.

Combine the walnuts, bread crumbs, grated rinds, baking powder, spices, and salt in a large mixing bowl. Beat the yolks with the sugar in the bowl of an electric mixer until thick and light in color. Add the vanilla and water to the egg yolk–sugar mixture; then stir in the walnut-spice mixture.

In a clean mixing bowl, beat the egg whites with the cream of tartar just until the whites hold their shape. Fold half the whites thoroughly into the batter. Fold in the remaining whites just until combined. Divide the batter evenly among the pans, and tap out any air bubbles. Bake at the center rack position of the oven for 25 to 30 minutes, until a cake tester comes out clean. Let cool completely in the pans. Turn out and carefully peel off the wax paper.

To make the brandy buttercream, beat the butter in the bowl of an electric mixer until it is smooth and creamy. Beat in the confectioners' sugar and salt, followed by the egg, vanilla, and enough brandy to make a good spreading consistency. Frost between the layers and over the top of the cake. Decorate with walnut halves.

M A K E S O N E 8 - I N C H 3 - L A Y E R C A K E

A spicy finale to have with coffee in front of the fire. The cake is large enough to provide seconds for everyone.

BUFFET BARBECUE

FOR **8**

Grilled Mustard-Coated Flank Steak

Vegetable Chili • **G**rilled Leeks

Savory Pecan Bread

Watermelon Slices

Ice-Cold Beer

Petite Sirah or Zinfandel

. . . .

The fragrance of grilled steak and hot chili will bring the sailors flocking in like seagulls. Ample portions are the only other necessity for sun-drenched, water-giddy adventurers.

Grilled Mustard-Coated Flank Steak

Flank steak responds to barbecuing much better than the more aristocratic cuts that require gentler treatment. Its flavor is not overwhelmed, and the juices are retained. Marinating and carving on the diagonal ensure tenderness.

1	**cup mixed mustards (any combination of mustard, such as prepared, whole-grained, Dijon-style, etc.)**
¼	**cup olive oil**
2	**teaspoons dried oregano**
2	**teaspoons dried thyme**
2	**teaspoons dried rosemary**
2	**teaspoons dried basil**
4	**medium garlic cloves, crushed or minced**
2	**flank steaks (1½ to 2 pounds each), all fat removed**

Combine the mustards with the olive oil, herbs, and garlic. Thickly coat the flank steaks with the mixture and refrigerate, covered, overnight. Remove from the refrigerator about 1 hour before cooking.

Prepare a barbecue and grill the flank steaks over a hot fire for 5 minutes on each side, until medium rare. Remove to a cutting board, cover with aluminum foil, and let rest for 10 minutes before slicing. Cut in thin diagonal slices across the grain and serve immediately.

SERVES 8

Vegetable Chili

Vegetable chili is a contradiction in terms to a purist, who will not admit even a bean to his chili. This one has hearty virtues, very evident in the mountains, and is a good accompaniment to the steak. Just don't let a Texan catch you at it.

- **1** pound red kidney beans, washed and drained (see Note)
- **1½** to 2 teaspoons salt
- **2** 1-pound cans of tomatoes, preferably Italian plum tomatoes
- **3** tablespoons vegetable oil
- **4** garlic cloves, peeled and minced
- **2** medium onions, peeled and chopped
- **2** celery stalks, cut into ½-inch dice
- **2** medium carrots, peeled and cut into ½-inch dice
- **2** small green peppers, cored, seeds and ribs removed, cut into ½-inch dice
- **¼** cup chopped fresh parsley
- **¼** cup dry red wine
- **2** tablespoons tomato paste
- **2** tablespoons freshly squeezed lemon juice
- **2** teaspoons chili powder
- **½** to 1 teaspoon ground cumin
   Dash of Tabasco sauce
   Salt and freshly ground black pepper, to taste
- **1** cup shredded Cheddar cheese

GARNISH
   Sour cream
   Minced chives or scallions

Put the kidney beans in a large pot, add 6 cups water, and soak the beans for 3 hours. Add another 2 cups water and the salt and bring to a boil. Reduce the heat to low and cook, covered, for 1 hour or more, until the beans are tender and most of the water has been absorbed. Set aside.

Strain the liquid from the canned tomatoes and reserve. Dice the tomatoes and set aside.

Heat the oil in a large skillet over moderate heat. Add the garlic and onions and cook, stirring, for 5 minutes, until the onions are tender. Add the tomatoes, celery, carrots, green peppers, parsley, wine, tomato paste, lemon juice, chili powder, cumin, Tabasco sauce, and salt and pepper. Cook, stirring often, for 20 minutes more, until the vegetables are tender.

Stir the vegetable mixture into the undrained cooked kidney beans and reheat. If too thick, thin with the reserved tomato liquid. If too thin, cook over medium high heat, uncovered, until thickened. Serve with shredded cheese. Garnish with sour cream sprinkled with minced chives or scallions.

NOTE: Two 27-ounce cans plus one 8-ounce can of good-quality kidney beans, drained, may be substituted. If so, adjust the amount of salt accordingly. You will most likely need to use all of the reserved tomato liquid in the vegetable mixture.

SERVES 8 AS A SIDE DISH OR 4 AS A MAIN COURSE

. . . .

Grilled Leeks

Splendidly contemporary in its simplicity, and an excellent foil for both the steak and the chili.

- **6** tablespoons (¾ stick) unsalted butter, melted
- **1½** tablespoons finely chopped mixed fresh herbs, such as tarragon, dill, and parsley
- **16** small leeks, preferably ¾ to 1 inch in diameter (see Note)
   Salt and freshly ground black pepper, to taste

Prepare a barbecue. Combine the melted butter with the mixed herbs and set aside.

To prepare the leeks, cut off the root, upper leaf tops, and any dried yellow skin. Make sure that 2 to 3 inches of green remains. Holding leafy side down, make a vertical slit down the middle of each leek, starting about 2 inches from the root and cutting down the length of the center. Repeat once or twice more to split the leek open. Rinse under cold running water until all the grit is washed off. Dry well.

When the barbecue coals are hot, place the leeks on the the grill. Brush generously with the herb butter, turning frequently. Watch carefully so they do not burn. Cook until the leeks are tender when pierced with a knife and the exteriors are lightly blackened, about 10 minutes. Sprinkle with salt and pepper. Serve immediately.

NOTE: If larger leeks are used, blanch first in boiling water for 3 to 5 minutes, until crisp-tender. Drain, refresh under cold water, and dry before grilling.

SERVES 8

Savory Pecan Bread

An unusual, interesting combination of flavors and textures. Unlike many nut breads, it is not sweet.

- **Vegetable oil**
- 2 **tablespoons finely ground pecans**
- 2 **packages active dry yeast**
- ½ **cup lukewarm water (105° to 115°)**
- **Pinch of sugar**
- 1½ **cups lukewarm milk (105° to 115°)**
- 9 **tablespoons unsalted butter, melted**
- 2 **teaspoons salt**
- 1 **tablespoon sugar**
- ½ **cup whole wheat flour**
- ½ **cup rye flour**
- 4½ **to 5½ cups unbleached all-purpose flour**
- 1 **cup finely chopped onion**
- 1 **cup toasted pecans, chopped**
- ¼ **cup unbleached all-purpose flour**
- 1 **egg white, slightly beaten**

Oil two 8-inch cake pans or baking sheets and sprinkle with ground pecans. Dissolve the yeast in the lukewarm water with a pinch of sugar and let sit for 5 to 10 minutes.

In the large bowl of an electric mixer, combine the lukewarm milk, 8 tablespoons melted butter, the salt, and 1 tablespoon sugar. Mix well. Add the yeast mixture and the whole wheat and rye flours and mix well. Add the unbleached flour, 1 cup at a time, until the dough comes together. Knead on a floured board for 8 to 10 minutes, until smooth and elastic, adding more flour if needed. Place in an oiled bowl, turning the dough to coat well, cover with a towel, and let rise in a warm place for 1½ to 2 hours.

Sauté the onion in the remaining 1 tablespoon melted butter. Let cool. On a floured board combine the toasted pecans, ¼ cup all-purpose flour, and the sautéed onion. Punch down the dough and knead in the pecan mixture a little at a time. Divide the dough in half and shape into 2 round loaves. Place in the prepared pans or on baking sheets. Cover and let rise for 45 minutes, until doubled. Meanwhile, preheat the oven to 400°. After the dough has risen, slash an X in the top of each round with a sharp knife, and brush with egg white.

Bake the breads for 30 to 40 minutes, until they sound hollow when tapped. For a crisper crust, place a pan of hot water on the bottom of the oven. Let cool on wire racks. Reheat before serving.

MAKES TWO 8-INCH ROUND LOAVES

The sun is in the west and sinking fast. It is time to get back to the blue water before it turns gray and cold and choppy. The meal was splendid.

SQUAW VALLEY

Cross-country skiing is less dangerous, perhaps easier to learn, but not easier to do than downhill skiing. One thinks of a pretty trail through snow-covered trees, but the trail has its ups as well as its downs, and no ski lift to help.

The appeal, of course, is simply beauty. Probably those ancients who had to slog great distances on snowshoes or skis felt the same exalted wonder at the first sight of a pristine field of snow, and looked back with the same pleasure at their lone tracks. Undoubtedly, the great mountain peaks standing silent and implacable in their robes of snow filled them with the same awe and respect and even joy the modern skier feels.

But although today's adventurer will sometimes find the trail a weary way, Squaw Valley has its cross-country skiing well in hand and as civilized as possible. Trips are tailored to skill and experience, trails graded for difficulty, and distances noted.

A picnic is definitely in order, whatever the challenge. It offers a chance to rest tired muscles and revive exhausted energies. And it is fun. This is wonderful food for a snowy occasion, wilderness or not. The soup is hearty, full of flavor and energy. Black bread and cheese have sustained many a traveler, but the bread was not often as fresh and fragrant as this, and few would have been so lucky as to have the virile Gorgonzola—perfect for the out-of-doors, and good with wine or cider. A fine Comice pear, at its best in early winter, is one of the great fruits of the West, and the perfect accompaniment to the meal.

CROSS-COUNTRY SKI PICNIC

FOR **8**

Beef, Lentil, and Split Pea Soup

Black Bread with Sweet Butter

Gorgonzola Cheese and Ripe Pears

Ice-Cold Beer with Soup

Sparkling Cider with Cheese and Fruit

. . . .

Beef, Lentil, and Split Pea Soup

Short ribs replace the more usual ham in this soup—which is almost a stew—to good effect. It is all the things it should be on a cold day: hearty, nourishing, warming, comforting.

- 2 **pounds short ribs of beef**
- 6 **tablespoons olive oil**
- 4 **tablespoons (½ stick) unsalted butter**
- ¼ **cup finely chopped onion**
- ¼ **cup finely chopped celery**
- ¼ **cup finely chopped carrot**
- ¼ **cup finely chopped parsnip**
- 2 **cups canned Italian tomatoes with basil, cut up, with their juice**
- ½ **pound dried lentils, washed and drained**
- ½ **pound dried split peas, washed and drained**
- 8 **cups (approximately) beef stock, preferably homemade (page 218)**
- ½ **teaspoon ground cumin**
  Salt and freshly ground black pepper, to taste

GARNISH
Wedges of lime and chopped fresh mint

Preheat the oven to 450°. Put the short ribs in an uncovered roaster and bake for 20 to 30 minutes, until browned, turning occasionally. Remove the meat from the roaster and set aside.

Meanwhile, heat the oil and butter in a large pot. Add the onion and sauté over medium high heat until golden brown. Add the celery, carrot, and parsnip and continue to cook for 3 to 4 minutes. Add the tomatoes and their juice, and reduce the heat to low. Simmer, uncovered, for 20 to 25 minutes. Add the lentils and peas to the pot and mix well. Add the browned short ribs and the beef stock, cumin, and salt and pepper. Bring to a boil, reduce the heat, and cook at a steady simmer, covered, for 1½ to 2 hours, until the lentils, split peas, and short ribs are tender and the soup has thickened. Adjust the seasonings.

Remove the ribs from the pot and cut the meat into serving-size pieces. Return the meat to the soup and reheat. Serve garnished with lime wedges and mint.

SERVES 8

Black Bread

Fresh and flavorful, this bread could be sandwiched with the cheese, ready to eat. Gorgonzola is one of the great Italian cheeses, strongly flavored, a wonderful foil for the soup.

- 4 **cups rye flour**
- 3 **cups unbleached all-purpose flour**
- 1 **teaspoon sugar**
- 2 **teaspoons salt**
- 2 **cups whole-bran cereal**
- 2 **to 3 tablespoons caraway seeds**
- 2 **packages active dry yeast**
- 2 **cups water**
- ½ **cup freshly brewed strong coffee**
- ¼ **cup distilled vinegar**
- ¼ **cup molasses**
- 1 **ounce unsweetened chocolate**
- 4 **tablespoons (½ stick) unsalted butter**

GLAZE
- 1 **teaspooon cornstarch mixed with ½ cup cold water**

Combine the rye and all-purpose flours. Mix 2⅓ cups of the flour mixture with the sugar, salt, cereal, caraway seeds, and yeast. Combine the remaining ingredients in a saucepan. Cook over low heat just until the butter and chocolate melt. Let cool to lukewarm.

Add the liquid mixture to the dry mixture and beat for 2 minutes. Mix in 2 cups of the mixed flour to make a thick dough. Turn out onto a generously floured board. Knead in the remaining flour, 1 cup at a time, for 10 minutes, until the dough is smooth and elastic. Put the dough in an oiled bowl, turning to coat all sides. Cover with a damp towel and let rise in a warm draft-free place for 1½ to 2 hours, until doubled.

Punch down the dough, divide it in half, and shape into two balls. Grease two 8-inch round cake pans and put a ball of dough in each. Cover and let rise in a warm draft-free place for 1 hour, until doubled.

Preheat the oven to 350°. Bake the loaves for 45 minutes, until the bread sounds hollow when tapped on the bottom. While the bread is baking, bring the cornstarch mixture to a boil and, stirring constantly, boil for 1 minute. When the bread is done, remove from the oven and brush the loaves with the glaze. Return the loaves to the oven for another 3 to 4 minutes. Remove from the pans and let cool on wire racks. Serve with unsalted butter.

MAKES 2 LOAVES

HIDDEN VALLEY

Two meals were arranged at a large working ranch in the well-named Hidden Valley. In the mountains between the civilizations of Malibu and the San Fernando Valley—and largely unknown to either—the little valley enjoys an almost secret life of country endeavor, and a sophisticated form of bucolic bliss.

Ranch life begets hearty appetites, and this is hearty food. Chicken and potato salad are traditional outdoor fare, but there is nothing traditional in this California treatment. Marinating and basting ensure juiciness in the chicken, whether served immediately or not, and rosemary adds fragrance. The red potato salad does not look like the usual potato salad, and does not taste like it either. Chives, parsley, and tarragon vinegar add freshness, and whipped cream adds richness. The green salad—with tomatoes, arugula, and fresh balls of mozzarella—is a garden of fresh tastes—and the baguettes stuffed with chopped green olives and prosciutto are wonderfully satisfying. Marinating the grapes in cognac, honey, and lemon juice gives them an interesting new flavor.

The more formal Sunday dinner was prepared to the lilt of an Irish brogue—with some California adjustments. Classic Irish stew, for example, is made with lamb, and only potatoes and onions, according to Theodora Fitzgibbons in *A Taste of Ireland*. But authenticity is no virtue in California cooking; one starts with an idea and runs with it. It is the result that counts. Beef also makes a fine stew; stout adds richness, as the Irish also know; and more vegetables simply make it more interesting. The potatoes never will be missed—especially as they turn up in another form as the Irish champ.

LUNCH ON THE LAWN

FOR **8**

Rosemary Chicken

Olive-Prosciutto Baguettes • **R**ed Potato Salad

Tomatoes, Arugula, and Bocconcini with
Green Herb Vinaigrette

Brandied Grapes

Sauvignon or Fumé Blanc

. . . .

Rosemary Chicken

If the chicken pieces are to be grilled away from home, they could be packed for the trip with the marinade, in self-closing plastic bags. (Plastic bags also simplify the marinating process.) The uncooked chicken should be kept in a cooler.

MARINADE
- 1 **to 2 tablespoons black peppercorns**
- ⅔ **cup freshly squeezed lemon juice**
- 6 **tablespoons olive oil**
- 1 **tablespoon salt**
- 3 **tablespoons chopped fresh rosemary or 1 tablespoon dried**

- 2 **3-pound chickens, whole and trussed, or cut into serving pieces**

Crush the peppercorns by using the bottom of a heavy skillet, a mortar and pestle, or a spice grinder. Combine with the lemon juice, olive oil, salt, and rosemary to make a marinade. Pour over the chickens or pieces, cover, and let sit 2 hours at room temperature, or refrigerated overnight. Turn once or twice to coat well.

Remove the chicken from the marinade, reserving the marinade for basting. If using whole chickens, preheat the oven to 425°. Place the chickens in roasting pan(s), breast side up. Basting occasionally with the reserved marinade, roast for 50 minutes, until the chickens are golden and the juices run clear.

If using pieces of chicken, place thighs and legs on a hot barbecue grill, skin side down, for 15 minutes. Add the breasts and wings and grill for 20 to 25 minutes more. Baste occasionally with the reserved marinade, turning the pieces to cook evenly. Remove from the grill when fork-tender and evenly browned.

Roasted or grilled chicken may be served hot or at room temperature.

SERVES 8

The table is set up under a tree, with a striped cloth, old, mix-matched silver, and white, wheat-patterned plates. An old earthenware pitcher holds bachelor buttons, straw flowers, and field grass.

The baguettes are a satisfying accompaniment to lunch.

Olive-Prosciutto Baguettes

A hearty and unusual bread. The better the prosciutto, the better the bread. Any good ham will do.

    1 envelope active dry yeast
    2 teaspoons sugar
    1 cup lukewarm water (105° to 115°)
       Yellow cornmeal
  2¼ cups bread flour plus 2 teaspoons for dusting
    1 cup (or more) unbleached all-purpose flour
    2 tablespoons vegetable oil
    ½ teaspoon salt
       Coarsely ground black pepper, to taste
    ¼ cup small Spanish green olives (with
       pimientos), drained, patted dry, and
       coarsely chopped
    6 ounces prosciutto, coarsely chopped
       Additional unbleached all-purpose flour

In a small bowl, dissolve the yeast and sugar in the lukewarm water. Let stand about 10 minutes, until the mixture is foamy. Oil a large bowl and set aside. Grease a double French bread pan or large baking sheet and sprinkle lightly with cornmeal. Set aside.

In another large bowl, combine 2¼ cups bread flour, 1 cup all-purpose flour, and the oil, salt, and pepper. Add the yeast mixture and stir until the dough is a rough mass and cleans the sides of the bowl. If dough is too wet, blend in additional all-purpose flour, a tablespoon at a time. Add the olives and prosciutto and mix thoroughly. Knead on a floured surface for 8 to 10 minutes, until smooth and elastic. Gather the dough into a ball and transfer to the oiled bowl; turn to coat the entire surface. Cover with a damp towel and let stand in a warm draft-free place for 1 hour, until doubled.

Turn the dough out onto a generously floured surface. Knead in enough additional all-purpose flour so that the dough is no longer sticky. Divide it in half. Roll each half into a 16-inch-long rectangle. Roll up into a long, narrow loaf to fit the baking pan. Pinch the ends and seam tightly closed. Transfer to the prepared pan or baking sheet, seam side down. Cover with a damp towel and let stand in a warm draft-free place for 45 minutes, until nearly doubled.

Position a rack in the center of the oven and preheat the oven to 425°. Sprinkle each baguette evenly with 1 teaspoon bread flour. Make several slashes in the top of each loaf. Bake for 25 to 30 minutes, until the loaves are a deep golden brown and sound hollow when tapped. Remove from the pan and transfer to a rack to cool.

MAKES 2 BAGUETTES

. . . .

Red Potato Salad

A pretty variation on an old faithful.

    3 pounds small red potatoes, unpeeled
    ¾ cup mayonnaise, preferably homemade
       (page 176)
    2 tablespoons tarragon vinegar
    ¾ teaspoon dry mustard
    ½ teaspoon salt, or to taste
    ¾ cup heavy cream, whipped
    ¼ cup snipped fresh chives
    ¼ cup minced fresh parsley
    ¼ cup finely minced shallots

GARNISH
    Additional snipped chives

Put the potatoes in a large pot of salted cold water. Bring to a boil and cook for 15 to 20 minutes, until tender but still firm. Drain and rinse under cold water. Refrigerate, covered, until chilled.

Cut the potatoes into ¾-inch cubes and set aside. In a medium bowl, blend the mayonnaise, vinegar, mustard, and salt. Fold in the whipped cream, chives, parsley, and shallots. Add the potatoes and fold gently to coat. Cover and refrigerate for at least 2 hours. To serve, sprinkle with chives.

SERVES 8

Tomatoes, Arugula, and Bocconcini with Green Herb Vinaigrette

We all say *arugula* in this country, although it is *rucola* in most of Italy. By either name this green is splendid. *Bocconcini* (little balls of fresh mozzarella, found in Italian markets and some supermarkets) means simply "mouth pleaser."

- **1 pound small tomatillos (Mexican green tomatoes), husked and cut in half**
- **2 pints cherry tomatoes**
- **4 bunches of arugula, stems removed**
- **1 pound bocconcini (little balls of fresh mozzarella cheese) or other fresh mozzarella, cut into small pieces**

GREEN HERB VINAIGRETTE
MAKES ABOUT 1 1/3 CUPS
- **1 egg**
- **2 tablespoons green herb mustard or Dijon-style mustard**
- **2 teaspoons balsamic vinegar**
- **1/4 cup Champagne vinegar**
- **1/2 teaspoon salt**
- **Freshly ground white pepper, to taste**
- **3/4 cup extra virgin olive oil**

Combine the tomatillos, cherry tomatoes, arugula, and bocconcini in a serving bowl. Set aside.

To make the dressing, combine the egg, mustard, vinegars, salt, and pepper in a small bowl. Slowly whisk in the oil, and continue to whisk until the dressing is emulsified.

Toss the salad with just enough dressing to coat.

SERVES 8

Pleasing to the eye and pleasing to the taste.

Grapes topped with crème fraîche and threads of caramel.

Brandied Grapes

Fruits were brandied in mid-eighteenth-century England to preserve them. In this very easy, very good recipe, the brandy gives extra flavor to the grapes. Caramelized grapes add an elegant touch.

- **6 tablespoons honey**
- **3 tablespoons Cognac or brandy**
- **1 1/2 teaspoons freshly squeezed lemon juice**
- **2 pounds seedless red and green grapes, washed and dried, with stems removed**

CARAMELIZED GRAPES (SEE NOTE)
- **1 cup sugar**
- **1/2 cup water**
- **Small clusters of grapes, washed and dried**

- **1 cup crème fraîche (see Note, page 53) or sour cream**

Blend the honey, Cognac or brandy, and lemon juice in a bowl. Add the grapes, cover, and refrigerate for at least 6 hours, or overnight, stirring occasionally.

To make the caramelized grapes, combine the sugar and water in a small saucepan, stirring to moisten the sugar. Bring to a boil over medium heat, stirring just until the sugar is dissolved. Wipe down the sides of the pan with a wet pastry brush. Continue to boil until the syrup is a medium-dark amber-colored caramel. Let cool slightly. Using a wooden skewer, dip grape clusters into the caramel to coat. Hold each cluster in the air so that threads are formed by the dripping caramel. Let dry on wax paper.

Serve in individual bowls topped with crème fraîche and garnished with caramelized grapes.

NOTE: Prepare the caramelized grapes as close as possible to serving time; do not refrigerate.

SERVES 8

SUNDAY DINNER

FOR **8**

Irish Beef Stew

Soda Bread

Champ

Rhubarb Crumble with Rich Custard Sauce

Charbono

. . . .

Irish Beef Stew

There are times when nothing is more satisfying than a stew. Like many stews, this one is even better the next day. Throw on a handful of chopped parsley for color just before serving.

Vegetable oil

3 pounds center-cut chuck steak or family steak, cut into 1½-inch pieces

Unbleached, all-purpose flour, seasoned with salt and pepper

3 onions, peeled and thinly sliced

1½ bottles Guinness Extra Stout

2 to 3 cups beef stock (or enough to cover), preferably homemade (page 218)

Salt and freshly ground black pepper, to taste

2 bay leaves

¾ pound carrots, peeled and cut into 1-inch × 1½-inch pieces

¾ pound turnips, peeled and cut into 1-inch × 1½-inch pieces

¾ pound parsnips, peeled and cut into 1-inch × 1½-inch pieces

Heat a thin layer of oil in a large sauté pan. Dip the meat in the seasoned flour and sauté in small quantities until golden brown. Remove and set aside. Add more oil if necessary and cook the onions for 10 minutes, until softened. Put the meat back in the pan and pour in the stout and enough stock to cover. Season with salt and pepper, and add the bay leaves. Cook, covered, over low heat for 1½ hours, until the meat is fairly tender. Add the vegetables, and adjust seasonings if necessary. Cook, covered, for ½ hour more, until the vegetables are tender.

The gravy should be thick and dark. If too thin, remove the meat and vegetables with a slotted spoon and cook the gravy down over moderately high heat to the desired consistency. Return the meat and vegetables to the pot and heat through.

SERVES 8

The warm soda bread is served in a basket, the Irish stew and champ in very old English hand-painted dishes. The full-blown roses come from the garden, and are the host's favorite flowers.

A hearty Irish feast.

Beef Stock

A darker stock can be made by browning the bones under the broiler or in a hot (425° to 450°) oven, then proceeding as directed. After straining and cooling it and removing the fat, you can reduce the stock as much you wish in a slow simmer.

3 **pounds beef shin or other meaty bones, sawed into several pieces**
3 **pounds meaty veal shank, sawed into several pieces**
3 **carrots, scrubbed and cut into 2-inch pieces**
1 **celery stalk with leaves, cut into 2-inch pieces**
1 **medium parsnip, scrubbed and coarsely chopped**
3 **medium leeks, white part only, well cleaned and sliced**
1 **bay leaf**
3 **sprigs of parsley**
½ **teaspoon dried thyme**
1 **teaspoon black peppercorns**

Put the meat into a stock pot or large kettle and add enough cold water to cover. Slowly bring to a boil. As froth starts to gather, remove it with a spoon, and continue to do so until it almost ceases to accumulate. Add the rest of the ingredients, adding more water if necessary so that all the ingredients are covered by 1 inch. Simmer partially covered for 6 hours or more, skimming as necessary. Do not stir. Add boiling water if necessary to keep the solids covered.

Strain and discard the solids, and let the stock cool. Refrigerate overnight and remove the congealed fat. Beef stock may be stored in the refrigerator for 3 to 4 days or it may be frozen.

MAKES 2 TO 3 QUARTS

Soda Bread

The classic bread of Ireland, traditionally cooked over a peat fire and offered with a cup of tea or a glass of stout. It makes delicious toast.

3 **cups whole wheat flour**
1½ **cups unbleached all-purpose flour**
2 **teaspoons salt**
1 **teaspoon baking soda**
½ **teaspoon baking powder**
2 **or more cups buttermilk**

Preheat the oven to 400°. Grease and flour a baking sheet.

Sift the dry ingredients into a bowl. Mix in the buttermilk with a wooden spoon, and add as much additional buttermilk as is necessary to form a slightly sticky dough. Knead on a floured board just long enough to form the dough into a round cake. Cut a cross about 4 inches long and 1 inch deep on top with a sharp knife, and place on the baking sheet. Bake for 30 to 40 minutes. When done, the bread should sound hollow when thumped on the bottom. If desired, wrap in a towel until cool to prevent a hard crust from forming. Serve warm with unsalted butter.

MAKES 1 ROUND LOAF

. . . .

Champ

Champ is simply mashed potatoes with more than the usual allotment of butter and scallions. They are made lighter in this recipe by processing through a ricer or food mill, but in Ireland they would be mashed in a large wooden tub with a heavy wooden pestle called a beetle. ("There was an old woman who lived in a lamp / She had no room to beetle her champ. . . .")

2 **pounds baking potatoes, peeled**
8 **tablespoons (1 stick) unsalted butter, cut into several pieces, at room temperature**
  Salt and freshly ground white pepper, to taste
2 **bunches of scallions, chopped**
  Milk

Put the potatoes in a pot of cold water and bring to a boil. Reduce the heat and cook for 20 to 25 minutes, until very tender. Drain thoroughly and return to the pot. Cover and continue to evaporate moisture by shaking the pot continuously for another couple of minutes. Put the potatoes through a ricer or food mill and mix in the butter and salt and pepper. Keep warm.

Put the scallions in a saucepan with just enough milk to cover. Bring to a boil and cook for 1 to 2 minutes. Mix the scallions and milk with the potatoes. Adjust the seasonings and serve immediately.

SERVES 8

. . . .

Rhubarb Crumble with Rich Custard Sauce

This simple, satisfying dessert is good with the custard sauce or, if you prefer, topped with whipped cream, plain cream, or vanilla ice cream.

3½ **pounds fresh rhubarb, washed, trimmed, and cut into 1-inch pieces**
1¼ **cups sugar**
2½ **cups unbleached all-purpose flour**
  1 **cup (2 sticks) unsalted butter, chilled and cut into pieces**

RICH CUSTARD SAUCE
  2 **cups heavy cream**
  6 **egg yolks**
½ **cup sugar**
  1 **teaspoon vanilla extract**

Preheat the oven to 400°. Butter a 3-quart ovenproof baking dish.

Put the rhubarb in a saucepan with ¾ cup sugar. Cover and cook for 10 minutes, until tender. Put the cooked rhubarb in the prepared dish.

Rhubarb crumble made elegant on a pretty plate.

Sift the flour and rub in the butter with your fingertips or a pastry blender. Add the remaining ½ cup sugar and sprinkle the mixture over the fruit. Bake for 30 minutes, until the top is nicely browned.

While the rhubarb is baking, make the custard sauce. Warm the cream in a saucepan. Whisk the egg yolks and sugar together until lightened and thick. Pour the warm cream over the egg-sugar mixture, combine, and return to the saucepan. Cook over low heat, stirring constantly, until slightly thickened. Remove from the heat, let cool slightly, then add the vanilla. Strain if desired.

Serve the crumble warm, with the custard sauce.

SERVES 8

INDEX

CREDITS

Recipe Donors

Terry Bell, Karen Berk, Helen Bing, Joan Burns, Rue Byars, Andrea Deane, Bonnie Erie, Catherine Firestone, Gerry Gilliland of Gilliland's, Kay Glass, Patsy Glass, Joan Graves, Nika Hazelton, Joan Hoien, Ed La Dou, Didier Lenders of The Lodge at Pebble Beach, Robert Levenstein, Bruce Marder and Bill Hufferd of West Beach Café and Rebecca's, Lydie Marshall, Barbara Nies, Betty Nowling, Wolfgang Puck of Spago and Chinois, Sandra Seltzer, Sylvia Schulman and Madam S. T. Ting Wong, Becky Smith, Joachim Splichel of Max au Triangle, Hollie Stotter, Vicki Weinert, Roy Yamaguchi of 385 North, Judy Zeidler

Art Museum Council Testing Committee

Terry Bell, Karen Berk, Helen Bing, Diane Bishop, Joan Burns, Rue Byars, Shirley Courage, Ina Dalsemer, Charlotte Davis, Carol Doumani, Bonnie Erie, Nancy Freedman, Barbara George, Kay Glass, Patsy Glass, Elaine Goldsmith, Sonia Goodman, Joan Graves, Claire Hammerman, Linda Hartwick, Audrey Hill, Eleanor Johnson, Joanne Keith, Ruth Kennedy, Suzanne Labiner, June Matsumoto, Clerimond McDaniel, Joan Nicholas, Betty Nowling, Jeanne Olsen, Devon Ortiz, Leona Palmer, Kitt Roberts, Merelie Robinson, Dory Soffer, Phyllis Wayne

Home and Yacht Owners

Gretchen and John Berggruen, Joan and Allan Burns, Stephen Chase, James Lee Costa, Carol and Roy Doumani, Catherine and Brooks Firestone, Jo Ann and Julian Ganz, Jr., Linda Gaede, Ellen and Ian Graham, Barbara and Robert Grant, Susan and Robert Maguire III, Vesta and Manouchehr Mobedshahi, Pat Montandon, Marguerite and Scott Moore, David H. Murdock, Harriet and George Pfleger, Olive and William Shannon, Debra and James Swinden, Glen Wilson, Ron Wilson, Miriam Wosk

Site Assistants and Special Friends

Betty Asher, Sharon Bates, Moya Bullis, Elizabeth Burns, Doris Coleman, Stuart Doan, Marie Ferguson, Meralee and Leonard Goldman, Emily Hunt, Joyce and Eugene Klein, Patrice Larroque, Rita Leinwand, Jacqueline and Hoyt Leisure, George Livermore, Joan and John Menkes, Dare Michos, Beverly and Chase Morsey, Peter Paanakker, Kevin Richards, Carole Saville, Becky and Peter Smith, Jill Spalding, Audrey and Barry Sterling, DeWain Valentine, Mili Wild, Laura Lee and Robert Woods, Jr.

Tableware and Flowers Contributors

Newport Beach
Neiman-Marcus, Kitchen Things

Los Angeles
Natural Selection; Katsu Restaurant; Functional Art; Nonesuch Gallery; Valentino; Montana Mercantile; Buddy's; By Design; Joyce Hundal Imports; Richard Mulligan; Murray & Olson, Florist; Slightly Crazed; Martha Ragland; Sydney de Jong; Joan Baizer

San Francisco
Gumps; Sue Fisher King; A Bed of Roses, Florist; Ronald James Antiques; Paul Bauer, Inc.; Tiffany & Co.

Pebble Beach
Flowers Limited

Carmel
Succulent Gardens, Allen & Co.

New York City
Wolfman Gold & Good Co.; Frank McIntosh shop at Henri Bendel; Lee Bailey shop at Henri Bendel; Dan Bleier Studio; Dean & DeLuca; Sointu Modern Design Shop; Crownford China